DATE DUE

MAY 2 1 1991	DEC 12 1998	
SEP 1 3 1992	OCT 18 1999	
OCT 1 9 1993	APR 29 2001	
MAR 19 1996	JAN 1 3 2002	
4/9		
APR 25 1996	OCT 03 2004	
	NOV 14 2004	
JUN 15 1996	FEB 09 2005	
OCT 27 1996		
DEC 12 1996		
DEC 30 1996		
APR 1 3 1997		
APR 07 1998		
12/31/02		

DEMCO 38-296

Modern Critical Interpretations

Geoffrey Chaucer's
The Knight's Tale

Modern Critical Interpretations

The Oresteia
Beowulf
The General Prologue to
  The Canterbury Tales
The Pardoner's Tale
The Knight's Tale
The Divine Comedy
Exodus
Genesis
The Gospels
The Iliad
The Book of Job
Volpone
Doctor Faustus
The Revelation of St.
  John the Divine
The Song of Songs
Oedipus Rex
The Aeneid
The Duchess of Malfi
Antony and Cleopatra
As You Like It
Coriolanus
Hamlet
Henry IV, Part I
Henry IV, Part II
Henry V
Julius Caesar
King Lear
Macbeth
Measure for Measure
The Merchant of Venice
A Midsummer Night's
  Dream
Much Ado About
  Nothing
Othello
Richard II
Richard III
The Sonnets
Taming of the Shrew
The Tempest
Twelfth Night
The Winter's Tale
Emma
Mansfield Park
Pride and Prejudice
The Life of Samuel
  Johnson
Moll Flanders
Robinson Crusoe
Tom Jones
The Beggar's Opera
Gray's Elegy
Paradise Lost
The Rape of the Lock
Tristram Shandy
Gulliver's Travels

Evelina
The Marriage of Heaven
  and Hell
Songs of Innocence and
  Experience
Jane Eyre
Wuthering Heights
Don Juan
The Rime of the Ancient
  Mariner
Bleak House
David Copperfield
Hard Times
A Tale of Two Cities
Middlemarch
The Mill on the Floss
Jude the Obscure
The Mayor of
  Casterbridge
The Return of the Native
Tess of the D'Urbervilles
The Odes of Keats
Frankenstein
Vanity Fair
Barchester Towers
The Prelude
The Red Badge of
  Courage
The Scarlet Letter
The Ambassadors
Daisy Miller, The Turn
  of the Screw, and
  Other Tales
The Portrait of a Lady
Billy Budd, Benito Cer-
  eno, Bartleby the Scriv-
  ener, and Other Tales
Moby-Dick
The Tales of Poe
Walden
Adventures of
  Huckleberry Finn
The Life of Frederick
  Douglass
Heart of Darkness
Lord Jim
Nostromo
A Passage to India
Dubliners
A Portrait of the Artist as
  a Young Man
Ulysses
Kim
The Rainbow
Sons and Lovers
Women in Love
1984
Major Barbara

Man and Superman
Pygmalion
St. Joan
The Playboy of the
  Western World
The Importance of Being
  Earnest
Mrs. Dalloway
To the Lighthouse
My Antonia
An American Tragedy
Murder in the Cathedral
The Waste Land
Absalom, Absalom!
Light in August
Sanctuary
The Sound and the Fury
The Great Gatsby
A Farewell to Arms
The Sun Also Rises
Arrowsmith
Lolita
The Iceman Cometh
Long Day's Journey Into
  Night
The Grapes of Wrath
Miss Lonelyhearts
The Glass Menagerie
A Streetcar Named
  Desire
Their Eyes Were
  Watching God
Native Son
Waiting for Godot
Herzog
All My Sons
Death of a Salesman
Gravity's Rainbow
All the King's Men
The Left Hand of
  Darkness
The Brothers Karamazov
Crime and Punishment
Madame Bovary
The Interpretation of
  Dreams
The Castle
The Metamorphosis
The Trial
Man's Fate
The Magic Mountain
Montaigne's Essays
Remembrance of Things
  Past
The Red and the Black
Anna Karenina
War and Peace

These and other titles in preparation

Modern Critical Interpretations

Geoffrey Chaucer's
The Knight's Tale

Edited and with an introduction by

Harold Bloom
Sterling Professor of the Humanities
Yale University

Chelsea House Publishers ◊ *1988*
NEW YORK ◊ NEW HAVEN ◊ PHILADELPHIA

© 1988 by Chelsea House Publishers,
a division of Chelsea House Educational Communications, Inc.

Introduction © 1988 by Harold Bloom

Printed and bound in the United States of America

10 9 8 7 6 5 4 3 2 1

∞ The paper used in this publication meets the minimum
requirements of the American National Standard for Permanence
of Paper for Printed Library Materials, Z39.48-1984

Library of Congress Cataloging-in-Publication Data
Geoffrey Chaucer's The knight's tale/edited and with an introduction
    by Harold Bloom.
    p.   cm. — (Modern critical interpretations)
    Bibliography: p.
    Includes index.
    Contents: Order and disorder/Charles Muscatine—Keeping
appointments we never made/E. Talbot Donaldson—The meaning of
Chaucer's Knight's tale/Douglas Brooks and Alastair Fowler—Tale
of civil conduct/Donald R. Howard—The struggle between noble
designs and chaos: the literary tradition of Chaucer's Knight's
tale/Robert W. Hanning—Sic et non: discarded worlds in The
knight's tale/F. Anne Payne—An opening: The knight's tale/
Helen Cooper—The first two poets of the Canterbury tales/C.
David Benson.
    ISBN 0-87754-907-9 (alk. paper)
    1. Chaucer, Geoffrey, d. 1400. Knight's tale. [1. Chaucer,
Geoffrey, d. 1400. Knight's tale.   2. English literature—History
and criticism.]   I. Bloom, Harold.   II. Series
PR1868.K63G46   1988
821'.1—dc19   87–27468
                                                                        CIP
                                                                        AC

Contents

Editor's Note

This book brings together a representative selection of the best modern critical interpretations of the Knight's Tale from the *Canterbury Tales* of Geoffrey Chaucer. The critical discussions are reprinted here in the chronological order of their original publication. I am grateful to Maria Carrig for her erudite assistance in editing this volume.

My introduction first considers Chaucer's experiential stance as a poet and then relates the Knight's Tale to the Knight's own narrative stance, which is the necessity to bear oneself with equanimity, since one must constantly keep appointments one has never made (to employ Talbot Donaldson's fine paraphrase of Chaucer).

Charles Muscatine begins the chronological sequence of criticism with his classic essay on Theseus as an idea of order in the Knight's Tale, after which the late Talbot Donaldson, the most Chaucerian of Chaucerians since G. K. Chesterton, sets forth the relation of the poem to *The Consolation of Philosophy* by Boethius.

The astrological context of the poem is learnedly expounded by Douglas Brooks and Alastair Fowler, while the late Donald R. Howard gives us a sense of Chaucer's own reservations towards the Knight's vision. Robert W. Hanning compares the poem to the *Thebiad* of Statius and the *Teseida* of Boccaccio and discusses the effect of Chaucer's tale being related by a professional soldier.

Boethius returns in F. Anne Payne's analysis of the Knight's Tale as a Menippean satire, after which Helen Cooper discusses the poem's structure in the context of medieval romances and of Boccaccio in particular. C. David Benson concludes this volume by contrasting the Knight's Tale with the Miller's Tale, demonstrating how reading them together adds to the very different literary power that each manifests.

Introduction

Chaucer is one of those great writers who defeat almost all criticism, an attribute he shares with Shakespeare, Cervantes, and Tolstoy. There are writers of similar magnitude—Dante, Milton, Wordsworth, Proust—who provoke inspired commentary (amidst much more that is humdrum), but Chaucer, like his few peers, has such mimetic force that the critic is disarmed and so is left either with nothing or with everything still to do. Much criticism devoted to Chaucer is merely historical, or even theological, as though Chaucer ought to be read as a supreme version of medieval Christianity. But I myself am not a Chaucer scholar, and so I write this introduction and edit this volume only as a general critic of literature and as a common reader of Chaucer.

Together with Shakespeare and a handful of the greater novelists in English, Chaucer carries the language further into unthinkable triumphs of the representation of reality than ought to be possible. The Pardoner and the Wife of Bath, like Hamlet and Falstaff, call into question nearly every mode of criticism that is now fashionable. What sense does it make to speak of the Pardoner or the Wife of Bath as being only a structure of tropes, or to say that any tale they tell has suspended its referential aspect almost entirely? The most Chaucerian and best of all Chaucer critics, E. Talbot Donaldson, remarks of the General Prologue to the *Canterbury Tales*:

> The extraordinary quality of the portraits is their vitality, the illusion that each gives the reader that the character being described is not a fiction but a person, so that it seems as if the poet has not created but merely recorded.

As a critical remark, this is the indispensable starting point for reading Chaucer, but contemporary modes of interpretation deny that such an illusion of vitality has any value. Last June, I walked through a park in Frankfurt, West Germany, with a good friend who is a leading French theorist of interpretation. I had been in Frankfurt to lecture on Freud; my friend had just arrived to give a talk on Joyce's *Ulysses*. As we walked, I remarked that Joyce's Leopold Bloom seemed to me the most sympathetic and affectionate person I had encountered in any fiction. My friend, annoyed and perplexed, replied that Poldy was *not* a person, and that my statement therefore was devoid of sense. Though not agreeing, I reflected silently that the difference between my friend and myself could not be reconciled by anything I could say. To him, *Ulysses* was not even persuasive rhetoric, but was a system of tropes. To me, it was above all else the personality of Poldy. My friend's deconstructionism, I again realized, was only another formalism, a very tough-minded and skeptical formalism. But all critical formalism reaches its limits rather quickly when fictions are strong enough. L. C. Knights famously insisted that Lady Macbeth's children were as meaningless a critical issue as the girlhood of Shakespeare's heroines, a view in which Knights followed E. E. Stoll who, whether he knew it or not, followed E. A. Poe. To Knights, Falstaff "is not a man, but a choric commentary." The paradox, though, is that this "choric commentary" is more vital than we are, which teaches us that Falstaff is neither trope nor commentary, but a representation of what a human being *might* be, if that person were even wittier than Oscar Wilde, and even more turbulently high-spirited than Zero Mostel. Falstaff, Poldy, the Wife of Bath: these are what Shelley called "forms more real than living man."

Immensely original authors (and they are not many) seem to have no precursors, and so seem to be children without parents. Shakespeare is the overwhelming instance, since he swallowed up his immediate precursor Christopher Marlowe, whereas Chaucer charmingly claims fictive authorities while being immensely in-debted to actual French and Italian writers and to Boccaccio in particular. Yet it may be that Chaucer is as much Shakespeare's great original as he was Spenser's. What is virtually without prece-dent in Shakespeare is that his characters *change themselves by ponder-ing upon what they themselves say*. In Homer and the Bible and Dante, we do not find sea changes in particular persons brought about by those persons' own language, that is, by the differences that individual diction and tone make as speech produces further speech. But the Pardoner and the Wife of Bath are well along the mimetic way that leads to Hamlet and Falstaff. What they say to others, and to themselves, partly reflects what they already are, but partly engenders also what they will be. And perhaps even more subtly and forcefully, Chaucer suggests ineluctable transformations going on in the Pardoner and the Wife of Bath through the effect of the language of the tales they choose to tell.

Something of this shared power in Chaucer and Shakespeare accounts for the failures of criticism to apprehend them, particularly when criticism is formalist, or too given over to the study of codes, conventions, and what is now called "language" but might more aptly be called applied linguistics, or even psycholinguistics. A critic addicted to what is now called the "priority of language over meaning" will not be much given to searching for meaning in persons, real or imagined. But persons, at once real *and* imagined, are the fundamental basis of the experiential art of Chaucer and Shakespeare. Chaucer and Shakespeare know, beyond knowing, the labyrinthine ways in which the individual self is always a picnic of selves. "The poets were there before me," Freud remarked, and perhaps Nietzsche ought to have remarked the same.

II

Talbot Donaldson rightly insists, against the patristic exegetes, that Chaucer was primarily a comic writer. This need never be qualified, if we also judge the Shakespeare of the two parts of *Henry the Fourth* to be an essentially comic writer, as well as Fielding, Dickens, and Joyce. "Comic writer" here means something very comprehensive, with the kind of "comedy" involved being more in the mode, say, of Balzac than that of Dante, deeply as Chaucer was indebted to Dante notwithstanding. If the Pardoner is fundamentally a comic figure, why then so is Vautrin. Balzac's hallucinatory "realism," a cosmos in which every janitor is a genius, as Baudelaire remarked, has its affinities with the charged vitalism of Chaucer's fictive world. The most illuminating exegete of the General Prologue to the *Canterbury Tales* remains William Blake, whose affinities with Chaucer were profound. This is the Blake classed by Yeats, in *A Vision,* with Rabelais and Aretino; Blake as a heroic vitalist whose motto was "Exuberance is Beauty," which is an apt Chaucerian slogan also. I will grant that the Pardoner's is a negative exuberance, and yet Blake's remarks show us that the Wife of Bath's exuberance has its negative aspects also.

Comic writing so large and so profound hardly seems to admit a rule for literary criticism. Confronted by the Wife of Bath or Falstaff or the suprahumane Poldy, how shall the critic conceive her or his enterprise? What is there left to be done? I grimace to think of the Wife of Bath and Falstaff deconstructed, or of having their life-augmenting contradictions subjected to a Marxist critique. The Wife of Bath and difference (or even "differance")? Falstaff and surplus value? Poldy and the dogma that there is nothing outside the text? Hamlet and Lacan's Mirror Phase? The heroic, the vitalizing pathos of a fully human vision, brought about through a supermimesis not of essential nature, but of human possibility, demands a criticism more commensurate with its scope and its color. It is a matter of aesthetic tact, certainly, but as Oscar Wilde taught us, that makes it truly a moral matter as well. What devitalizes the Wife of Bath, or Falstaff, or Poldy, tends at last to reduce us also.

III

That a tradition of major poetry goes from Chaucer to Spenser and Milton and on through them to Blake and Wordsworth, Shelley and Keats, Browning and Tennyson and Whitman, Yeats and Stevens, D. H. Lawrence and Hart Crane is now widely accepted as a critical truth. The myth of a Metaphysical countertradition, from Donne and Marvell through Dryden, Pope, and Byron on to Hopkins, Eliot, and Pound, has been dispelled and seen as the Eliotic invention it truly was. Shakespeare is too large for any tradition, and so is Chaucer. One can wonder if even the greatest novelists in the language—Richardson, Austen, George Eliot, Dickens, Henry James, and the Mark Twain of *Huckleberry Finn* (the one true rival to *Moby-Dick* and *Leaves of Grass* as *the* American book or Bible), or Conrad, Lawrence, Joyce, and Faulkner in this century—can approach Shakespeare and Chaucer in the astonishing art of somehow creating fictions that are more human than we generally are. Criticism, perhaps permanently ruined by Aristotle's formalism, has had little hope of even accurately describing this art. Aristophanes, Plato, and Longinus are apter models for a criticism more adequate to Chaucer and to Shakespeare. Attacking Euripides, Aristophanes, as it were, attacks Chaucer and Shakespeare in a true prolepsis, and Plato's war against Homer, his attack upon mimesis, prophesies an unwaged war upon Chaucer and Shakespeare. Homer and Euripides after all simply are not the mimetic scandal that is constituted by Chaucer and Shakespeare; the *inwardness* of the Pardoner and Hamlet is of an order different from that of Achilles and Medea. Freud himself does not catch up to Chaucer and Shakespeare; he gets as far as Montaigne and Rousseau, which indeed is a long journey into the interior. But the Pardoner *is* the interior and even Iago, even Goneril and Regan, Cornwall and Edmund, do not give us a fiercer sense of intolerable resonance on the way down and out. Donaldson subtly observes that "it is the Pardoner's particular tragedy that, except in church, every one can see through him at a glance." The profound phrase here is "except in church." What happens to, or better yet, *within* the Pardoner when he preaches in church? Is that not parallel to asking what happens within the dying Edmund when he murmurs, "Yet Edmund was beloved," and thus somehow is moved to make his belated, futile attempt to save Cordelia and Lear? Are there any critical codes or methods that could possibly help us to sort out the Pardoner's more-than-Dostoevskian intermixture of supernatural faith and preternatural chicanery? Will semiotics or even Lacanian psycholinguistics anatomize Edmund for us, let alone Regan?

Either we become experiential critics when we read Chaucer and Shakespeare, or in too clear a sense we never read them at all. "Experiential" here necessarily means humane observation both of others and of ourselves, which leads to testing such observations in every context that indisputably is relevant. Longinus is the ancestor of such experiential criticism, but its masters are Samuel Johnson, Hazlitt and Emerson, Ruskin, Pater, and Wilde. A century gone mad on method has given us no critics to match these, nor are they likely to come again soon, though we still have Northrop Frye and Kenneth Burke, their last legitimate descendants.

IV

Mad on method, we have turned to rhetoric, and so much so that the best of us, the late Paul de Man, all but urged us to identify literature with rhetoric, so that criticism perhaps would become again the rhetoric of rhetoric, rather than a Burkean rhetoric of motives, or a Fryean rhetoric of desires. Expounding the Nun's Priest's Tale, Talbot Donaldson points to "the enormous rhetorical elaboration of the telling" and is moved to a powerful insight into experiential criticism:

> Rhetoric here is regarded as the inadequate defense that mankind erects against an inscrutable reality; rhetoric enables man at best to regard himself as a being of heroic proportions—like Achilles, or like Chauntecleer—and at worst to maintain the last sad vestiges of his dignity (as a rooster Chauntecleer is carried in the fox's mouth, but as a hero he rides on his back), rhetoric enables man to find significance both in his desires and in his fate, and to pretend to himself that the universe takes him seriously. And rhetoric has a habit, too, of collapsing in the presence of simple common sense.

Yet rhetoric, as Donaldson implies, if it is Chaucer's rhetoric in particular, can be a life-enhancing as well as a life-protecting defense. Here is the heroic pathos of the Wife of Bath, enlarging existence even as she sums up its costs in one of those famous Chaucerian passages that herald Shakespearean exuberances to come:

> But Lord Crist, whan that it remembreth me
> Upon my youthe and on my jolitee,
> It tikleth me aboute myn herte roote—
> Unto this day it dooth myn herte boote
> That I have had my world as in my time.
> But age, allas, that al wol envenime,
> Hath me biraft my beautee and my pith—
> Lat go, farewel, the devel go therewith!
> The flour is goon, ther is namore to telle:
> The bren as I best can now moste I selle;
> But yit to be right merye wol I fonde.
>
> (E. T. Donaldson, 2d ed.)

The defense against time, so celebrated as a defiance of time's revenges, is the Wife's fierce assertion also of the will to live at whatever expense. Rhetorically, the center of the passage is in the famously immense reverberation of her great cry of exultation and loss, "That I have had my world as in my time," where the double "my" is decisive, yet the "have had" falls away in a further intimation of mortality. Like Falstaff, the Wife is a grand trope of pathos, of life defending itself against every convention that would throw us into death-in-life. Donaldson wisely warns us that "pathos, however, must not be allowed to carry the day," and points to the coarse vigor of the Wife's final benediction to the tale she has told:

> And Jesu Crist us sende
> Housbondes meeke, yonge, and fresshe abedde—
> And grace t'overbide hem that we wedde.
> And eek I praye Jesu shorte hir lives
> That nought wol be governed by hir wives,
> And olde and angry nigardes of dispence—
> God sende hem soone a verray pestilence!

Blake feared the Wife of Bath because he saw in her what he called the Female Will incarnate. By the Female Will, Blake meant the will of the natural woman *or* the natural man, a prolepsis perhaps of Schopenhauer's rapacious Will to Live or Freud's "frontier concept" of the drive. Chaucer, I think, would not have quarreled with such an interpretation, but he would have scorned Blake's dread of the natural will or Schopenhauer's horror of its rapacity. Despite every attempt to assimilate him to a poetry of belief, Chaucer actually surpasses even Shakespeare as a celebrant of the natural heart, while like Shakespeare being beyond illusions concerning the merely natural. No great poet was less of a dualist than Chaucer was, and nothing makes poetry more difficult for critics, because all criticism is necessarily dualistic.

The consolation for critics and readers is that Chaucer and Shakespeare, Cervantes and Tolstoy, persuade us finally that everything remains to be done in the development of a criticism dynamic and comprehensive enough to represent such absolute writers without reduction or distortion. No codes or methods will advance the reading of Chaucer. The critic is thrown back upon herself or himself and upon the necessity to become a vitalizing interpreter in the service of an art whose burden is only to carry more life forward into a time without boundaries.

V

The Knight's Tale is a chivalric romance, or purports to be; it is as much genial satire as romance, a triumph of Chaucer's comic rhetoric, monistic and life-enhancing. Talbot Donaldson charmingly sums up the poem's ethos as being rather more Stoic than Christian: "No matter how hard we look, we cannot hope to see why Providence behaves as it does; all we can do is our best, making a virtue of necessity, enjoying what is good, and remaining cheerful." Applied to most other authors, Donaldson's comments might seem banal. Chaucer's overwhelming representation of an immediate reality, in which we ride with the protagonists, enjoy what is good, and certainly become more cheerful, gives Donaldson's amiable observations their edge of precision. Since Chaucer the Pilgrim rides along with us, allowing his own narrative voice full scope, despite the authority of his storytellers, we hear more than the Knight's tonalities in the telling of his tale.

Donald R. Howard, admirably setting forth "the idea" of the *Canterbury Tales,* the totality of its vision, reminds us that Chaucer himself may be in a skeptical stance towards the Knight's Tale, if only because the voice of the Knight, as narrator, is so much at variance with Chaucer's larger idea or vision:

> And the work, because of this idea, discourages us from assenting to the tales, from giving them credence. Almost every tale is presented in circumstances which discredit it. Even the Knight's Tale, a high-minded story told by an ideal figure, gives us reason to approach it skeptically. In it . . . Chaucer permits his own voice to intrude upon the Knight's. These ironic intrusions may discredit the tale itself, or the Knight, or the style and manner of its telling, or the cultural and literary tradition it represents. However explained, this ironic element raises questions in the reader's mind which the tale never settles. In other instances what we know about the pilgrim raises such questions. The Miller's Tale parodies the Knight's and holds some of its values up to ridicule; but the Miller does not get the last word and there is no reason to think Chaucer sided with him more than another—he is, we are told, a drunk and a churl. Besides, the Reeve's tale "quits" the Miller and his tale, discredit-

ing both with another churlish viewpoint. Tales discredit each other, as with the Friar and Summoner. The Nun's Priest subtly discredits the Monk's tale and other tales which have preceded it. Whole groups of tales discredit one another by presenting various viewpoints in conflict— the sequence Knight-Miller-Reeve is an example, as is the "marriage group."

Talbot Donaldson places a particular emphasis upon one crucial couplet of the Knight's:

> It is ful fair a man to bare him evene,
> For alday meeteth men at unset stevene.

I remember walking once with the late and much mourned Donaldson, on an ordinary evening in New Haven, and hearing him quote that couplet, and then repeat his own superb paraphrase of it: "It is a good thing for a man to bear himself with equanimity, for one is constantly keeping appointments one never made." That certainly seems the Knight's ethos, and may have been Chaucer's, and doubtless does reflect *The Consolation of Philosophy* of Boethius. Yet Chaucer, as Donaldson helped teach us, is a very great comic writer—like Rabelais, Cervantes, Shakespeare. As a poet, Chaucer is larger than any formulation we can bring to bear upon him, and, again like Shakespeare, he tends to transcend genres also.

F. Anne Payne argues cogently that "the Knight's Tale, a philosophical parody with the *Consolation* and the romance as its models, belongs to the seriocomic tradition of Menippean satire." Less a genre than a grab bag, Menippean satire is essentially typified by Lucian, whose dialogues turn their mockery in several directions at once. Lucian is less a satirist than an extreme ironist, who exploits precisely that aspect of irony that the late Paul de Man termed "a permanent parabasis of meaning." The irony of irony, with its destruction of any fixed meaning, is the irony of the Knight's Tale, where nothing can be settled and much must be accepted. Donaldson, in his splendid final book, *The Swan at the Well: Shakespeare Reading Chaucer,* relates the irony of romantic love in *A Midsummer Night's Dream* to the irony of the Knight's Tale. Puck's "Lord, what fools these mortals be" falls short of the irony of Chaucer's Theseus: "who maie be a foole, but if he love?" The destruction of friendship by love, Chaucer's overt story, is itself

Chaucer's metaphor for the dispersion of meaning by a love of philosophical disputation, which the Knight's Tale converts into a mockery. That must be why Shakespeare based his own Theseus more on Chaucer's Knight than on Chaucer's Theseus. The Knight is no philosopher but rather a chivalric skeptic, and so is Shakespeare's Theseus, who like the Knight will not go beyond his own experience.

Though the Knight's skepticism does not extend to his own tale-telling, there is always a remarkable gap between the complexity of his narrative and his own insistence that it is all a quite simple if rather sad matter. Donaldson compares this stance to that of the Nun's Priest, who blandly urges us to take the pith of his tale while ignoring its rhetorical reverberations, that alone give it power and universality. The Knight has tied up generations of Chaucerians with his famous red herring of a moral question:

> You loveres axe I now this questioun:
> Who hath the worse, Arcite or Palamoun?

As Donaldson remarks, the question is wrong because there is no authentic difference between the two love-crazed worthies. The Knight may be no Chaucerian ironist, but the gap between the Knight's experience of life and that of most among us necessarily and ironically defeats every attempt we could make to answer the question, unless indeed we qualify as experiential critics. No Formalist or method-based reading will be able to turn the Knight's question into its implied realization, which is that all of us must confront and absorb the possible worst, however unlooked-for and undeserved.

Order and Disorder

Charles Muscatine

A reasonable sympathy with conventionalism requires our understanding that the experience of the idealizing imagination is no less
varied than that of realistic observation, and no less true. If the
themes of most of Chaucer's conventional poems seem to converge
toward the single point of recognizing supernal values in human
affairs, the nature of the pointing differs with each poem. We do
not read Chaucer, after all, for his philosophical conclusions, but
for his workings-out, his poetry. Similarly, if tradition seems to
codify Chaucer's poetry according to a fixed number of general
forms in a defined area of style, the particular structure and local
style of each poem are unique.

Chaucer's conventionalism should neither be dismissed nor
taken for granted. The criticism of the Knight's Tale has long
suffered from both of these errors. The trouble has been in the
kinds of assumptions brought to the poem, in an attention to its
poor dramatics rather than its rich symbolism, to its surface rather
than its structure. The poem is nominally a romance, adapted from
Boccaccio's *Teseida*. The plot concerns the rivalry of Palamon and
Arcite, Theban knights, who while they are imprisoned by Duke
Theseus fall in love with his fair kinswoman, Emilye. Arcite is
released from prison and Palamon escapes; they finally fight for
Emilye's hand in a tournament. Arcite wins, but at the moment of

From *Chaucer and the French Tradition: A Study in Style and Meaning*. © 1957 by the
Regents of the University of California, © 1985 by Charles Muscatine. University
of California Press, 1957.

victory, in a supernaturally inspired accident, he is thrown from his horse and thereafter dies. After a period of mourning, Palamon marries Emilye. This plot has been taken to be the poem's main feature; but unless we wish to attribute to Chaucer an unlikely lapse of skill or taste, it will not sustain very close scrutiny. The "characterization" of Palamon and Arcite has been widely invoked as a key to the poem. In one view the two knights have quasi-allegorical status, representing the Active Life versus the Contemplative Life. But there is little agreement upon which knight is actually the more "contemplative" or the more admirable: if Palamon, the ending is poetic justice; if Arcite, it is irony. The existence of any significant characterization in the poem has been seriously questioned [by J. R. Hulbert]:

> In the *Teseide* there is one hero, Arcita, who loves and is eventually loved by Emilia, a young woman characterized by a natural coquetry, an admiration for a good-looking young knight, and love and sympathy for the wounded hero. Palemone is a secondary figure, necessary to the plot because he brings about the death of Arcita. The story is a tragedy, caused by the mistake of Arcita in praying to Mars rather than to Venus. In Chaucer's story there are two heroes, who are practically indistinguishable from each other, and a heroine, who is merely a name. In the Italian poem it is possible to feel the interest in hero and heroine which is necessary if one is to be moved by a story. . . . In Chaucer's version, on the other hand, . . . it is hard to believe that anyone can sympathize with either hero or care which one wins Emelye.

In this approach the lack of characterization is the story's greatest weakness; what remains is merely an elaborate and now archaic game:

> Chaucer saw in the *Teseide* a plot which, with some alterations, could be used effectively to present one of those problems of love which the votaries of courtly love enjoyed considering . . . which of two young men, of equal worth and with almost equal claims, shall (or should) win the lady? Stated in such simple terms, the problem

may seem foolish, but to readers who could be interested in such questions of love . . . this problem would be no doubt poignant. . . . Obviously in so far as the ideas of courtly love have passed into oblivion since the middle ages, narratives in which they are basic cannot appeal to modern taste.

Long ago, Root suggested the possibility that the poem was not written under the assumptions of naturalism:

> If we are to read the *Knight's Tale* in the spirit in which Chaucer conceived it, we must give ourselves up to the spirit of romance; we must not look for subtle character-ization, nor for strict probability of action; we must de-light in the fair shows of things, and not ask too many questions. Chaucer can be realistic enough when he so elects; but here he has chosen otherwise. . . . It is not in the characterization, but in the description, that the great-ness of the *Knight's Tale* resides. . . . [It] is preeminently a web of splendidly pictured tapestry, in which the eye may take delight, and on which the memory may fondly linger.

Root's conclusion shares in the general critical distrust of the poem; while recognizing its texture he depreciates its meaning, as if these rich materials could not at the same time be the carefully chosen, well-ordered machinery of serious poetry. Generations of readers have made this the most perennially valued of the tales. But neither Root's nor the naturalistic interpretations begin to suggest the depth and complexity which one would expect to find in a work with such a reputation. Now although it is not always neces-sary to proceed inductively from style to reach a satisfactory inter-pretation of a poem, the method is sometimes useful in making clear certain assumptions with which the poem should be approached. In the Knight's Tale, furthermore, form and style are so functional that they point directly to the meaning.

The pace of the story is deliberately slow and majestic. Ran-dom references to generous periods of time make it chronologically slow. Though Chaucer omits a great deal of the tale originally told by Boccaccio in the *Teseida,* he frequently resorts to the rhetorical device of *occupatio* to summarize in detail events or descriptions in such a way as to shorten the story without lessening its weight and impressiveness. Further, there is an extraordinary amount of rhetorical *descriptio* in the poem, all of which slows the narrative. The description of the lists is very detailed, and placed so as to give the impression that we are present at their construction, an operation that appears to consume the full fifty weeks that Theseus allows for it. The narrator's repetitious "saugh I," and his closing remark, "Now been thise lystes maad" (l. 2089, F. N. Robinson, 1st ed.), cooperate to this effect.

We can hardly fail to note, too, that a great deal of this descriptive material has a richness of detail far in excess of the demands of the story. At first glance, at least, many passages appear to be irrelevant and detachable. For example, we have sixty-one lines of description of Emetrius and Lygurge; yet so far as the action of the poem is concerned, these two worthies do practically nothing.

Like the descriptions and narrator's comments, the direct discourse in the tale contributes to its slowness. There is virtually no rapid dialogue. Speeches of twenty-five or thirty verses are normal, and one, the final oration of Theseus, takes more than a hundred. More than length, however, the nondynamic *quality* of the speeches is characteristic of the whole poem's style. Many of them have only a nominal value as action or as the instruments to action. Formal, rhetorical structure, and a function comparatively unrelated to the practical necessities of the dramatic situation are the rule. This is true even where the speech is addressed to another character. For instance, when old Saturn is badgered by his granddaughter Venus to aid her in her conflict with Mars, he replies as follows:

> "My deere doghter Venus," quod Saturne,
> "My cours, that hath so wyde for to turne,
> Hath moore power than woot any man.
> Myn is the drenchyng in the see so wan;
> Myn is the prison in the derke cote;
> Myn is the stranglyng and hangyng by the throte,
> The murmure and the cherles rebellyng,
> The groynynge, and the pryvee empoysonyng;
> I do vengeance and pleyn correccioun,
> Whil I dwelle in the signe of the leoun.
> Myn is the ruyne of the hye halles,

> The fallynge of the toures and of the walles
> Upon the mynour or the carpenter.
> I slow Sampsoun, shakynge the piler;
> And myne be the maladyes colde,
> The derke tresons, and the castes olde;
> My lookyng is the fader of pestilence.
> Now weep namoore."
>
> (l. 2453ff.)

And finally, the rest of the speech, a mere eight verses, is devoted to promising Venus his aid. We can safely assume that Venus knows all about her grandfather. The long, self-descriptive introduction, therefore, must have some function other than the dramatic.

Going on now to the nature of the action, we find that while the chivalric aspects of the scene are described with minute particularity, there is very little in the Knight's Tale of the intimate and distinctive details of look, attitude, and gesture that mark some of Chaucer's more naturalistic poems. It is replete with conventional stage business. There are swoons and cries, fallings on knees, and sudden palenesses; there is a symphony of howls, wails, and lamentations.

When we look at the form in which these materials are organized, we find symmetry to be its most prominent feature. The unity of the poem is based on an unusually regular ordering of elements. The character grouping is symmetrical. There are two knights, Palamon and Arcite, in love with the same woman, Emilye. Above the three and in a position to sit in judgment, is the Duke Theseus, who throughout the poem is the center of authority and the balance between the opposing interests of the knights. In the realm of the supernatural, each of the knights and the lady has a patron deity: Venus, Mars, and Diana. The conflict between Venus and Mars is resolved by the elder Saturn, with no partiality toward either. In the tournament each knight is accompanied by one hundred followers headed by a particularly notable king, on one side Lygurge, on the other Emetrius:

> In al the world, to seken up and doun,
> So evene, withouten variacioun,
> There nere swiche compaignyes tweye;
> For there was noon so wys that koude seye
> That any hadde of oother avauntage

> Of worthynesse, ne of estaat, ne age,
> So evene were they chosen, for to gesse.
> And in two renges faire they hem dresse.
>
> (l. 2587ff.)

This arrangement of the two companies *in two renges* is one of many details of symmetry of scene and action in the poem. At the very beginning we find a uniformly clad company "of ladyes, tweye and tweye, / Ech after oother" (l. 898). When Palamon and Arcite are found in the heap of bodies at Thebes, they are "liggynge by and by, / Bothe in oon armes" (l. 1011). We find that they are cousins "of sustren two yborn" (l. 1019).

In the scene following the discovery of Emilye, each offers a lyric on the subject (ll. 1104ff., 1118ff.). When Arcite is released from prison, each delivers a complaint in which even the vocabulary and theme are symmetrical:

> "O deere cosyn Palamon," quod he,
> "Thyn is the victorie of this aventure."
>
> (l. 1234f.)

> "Allas," quod he, "Arcita, cosyn myn,
> Of al oure strif, God woot, the fruyt is thyn."
>
> (l. 1281f.)

In the second part, the narrator divides his attention between them, in alternate descriptions; and in the fight subsequent to their meeting they are evenly matched:

> Thou myghtest wene that this Palamon
> In his fightyng were a wood leon,
> And as a crueel tigre was Arcite.
>
> (l. 1655ff.)

Theseus appears, "And at a stert he was bitwix hem two" (l. 1705). He sets the conditions of the tournament in round numbers: " 'And this day fifty wykes, fer ne ner, / Everich of you shal brynge an hundred kynghtes' " (ll. 1850–51). In the third part the narrator describes the making of lists, in the same place as where the first fight occurs. The lists are circular in shape, a mile in circumference. They are entered from east and west by identical marble gates. The altars or temples of Mars and Venus are situated above these gates.

Northward (and equidistant from the other two, no doubt) is the *oratorie* of Diana. The three temples are described in succession, and each description is subdivided in the same way: first the wall-painting with its allegorical figures, and then the statue of the deity itself.

The symmetry of description continues with parallel accounts of the two rival companies, each containing a portrait of the leading king (ll. 2117–89). Then follow the prayers of the principals: Palamon to Venus, Emilye to Diana, Arcite to Mars. The prayers are made in careful order at the hours dedicated by astrology to those deities, and each prayer is answered by some supernatural event. Internally, too, the three prayers show a striking similarity of design, each beginning with rhetorical *pronominatio* and continuing with a reference to the deity's relations with the opposite sex, a self-description by the speaker, a humble assertion of incompetence, a request for assistance, and a promise to worship. The spectators enter the lists and are seated in order of rank. The combatants, Palamon and Arcite, with banners white and red respectively, enter the field through the gates of Venus and Mars.

After Arcite's death, his sepulcher is described. It is erected "ther as first Arcite and Palamoun / Hadden for love the bataille hem bitwene" (ll. 2858–59). This is also where the lists were built. The funeral procession, like the procession to the lists, is characterized by precise order, and the details of the funeral are full of the same kind of ordering:

> the Grekes, with an huge route,
> Thries riden al the fyr aboute
> Upon the left hand, with a loud shoutynge,
> And thries with hir speres claterynge;
> And thries how the ladyes gonne crye.
>
> (l. 2951ff.)

Further elements in the poem's symmetry of structure and scene could readily be brought forward.

Chaucer's modifications of the *Teseida* seem to have been made precisely in the interest of the kind of organization I am describing. By selection and addition he produced a poem much more symmetrical than its source. Chaucer even regularizes the times and places of the incidents in Boccaccio. He adds the character Emetrius, the parallel descriptions of Emetrius and Lygurge, and the description of Diana's temple. His crowning modification is the equalization of Palamon and Arcite.

These general and inescapable observations on the nature of the poem make clear how it must be approached. The symmetry of scene, action, and character grouping, the slow pace of the narrative and the large proportion of static description, the predominantly rhetorical kind of discourse—along with a lack of subtle discrimination in the stage business—all indicate that the tale is not the best kind in which to look for either delicate characterization or the peculiar fascination of an exciting plot. Subtle delineation of character is neither called for in the poem's design nor possible of achievement through the technical means Chaucer largely employs. There is neither rapid dialogue, nor psychological analysis, nor delicate and revelatory "business" in the poem. Nor does the Knight's Tale amount to much as plot and story interest go. Its value depends little on the traits that make a good story: a swift pace, suspense, variety, intrigue. Its main events are forecast long before they occur. The structure of the poem, indeed, works against story interest. Symmetry in character grouping, movement, time and place, supports the leisurely narrative and description in producing an overall sense of rest and deliberateness. The general intention indicated by the poem's materials and structure lies in a different direction. Its grouping and action, rather than existing for any great interest in themselves, seem constantly to point to a nonrepresentational, symbolic method. There is a decisive correlation of all its elements on this level.

The Knight's Tale is essentially neither a story nor a static picture, but rather a sort of poetic pageant. Its design expresses the nature of the noble life,

> That is to seyn, trouthe, honour, knyghthede,
> Wysdom, humblesse, estaat, and heigh kynrede,
> Fredom, and al that longeth to that art.
>
> (l. 2789ff.)

The story is immediately concerned with those two noble activities, love and chivalry, but even more important is the general tenor of the noble life, the pomp and ceremony, the dignity and power, and particularly the repose and assurance with which the exponent of nobility invokes order. Order, which characterizes the structure of the poem, is also the heart of its meaning. The society depicted is one in which form is full of significance, in which life is conducted at a dignified, processional pace, and in which life's pattern is itself a reflection, or better, a reproduction, of the order of the universe. And what gives this conception of life its perspective, its depth and seriousness, is its constant awareness of a formidably antagonistic element—chaos, disorder—which in life is an ever-threatening possibility, even in the moments of supremest assuredness, and which in the poem falls across the pattern of order, being clearly exemplified in the erratic reversals of the poem's plot, and deeply embedded in the poem's texture.

The descriptive sections of the tale support this interpretation perfectly, not only in the long passages that come immediately to mind, but also in the short flights that interrupt the narrative more than is warranted by what little information they add to the mere story. By contributing to currents that run continuously throughout the poem—currents that make up the main stream of the noble life—these superficially "irrelevant" descriptions achieve a secure position in the poem's pattern, and ultimately contribute in an important way to its meaning.

The portraits of Emetrius and Lygurge, for instance, have this kind of poetic relevance although their contribution to the surface narrative is slight. Emetrius has "A mantelet upon his shulder hangynge, / Bret-ful of rubyes rede as fyr sparklynge" (ll. 2163–64). Lygurge wears

> A wrethe of gold, arm-greet, of huge wighte,
> Upon his heed, set ful of stones brighte,
> Of fyne rubyes and of dyamauntz.
>
> (l. 2145ff.)

Unlike the portraits in the General Prologue, here the imagery is organized around no three-dimensional conception of personality; it is conventional, framed in the flat, to express the magnificence that befits nobility. I have noted that after all the description of these two kings they hardly figure in the narrative. The inference, however, is not that the portraits are a waste and an excrescence, "merely decorative," but that they perform a function that is not directly related to the action and is independent of the question of character. They contribute first to the poem's general texture, to the element of richness in the fabric of noble life. More specifically, Chaucer solves the problem of describing the rival companies by describing their leaders; not Palamon and Arcite, but their supporting kings. Their varicolored magnificence, like Theseus's banner, makes the whole field glitter up and down—black, white, yellow, red, green, and gold. Their personal attributes—the trumpet voice of Emetrius, the great brawn of Lygurge, their looks, like lion and griffin—give both a martial quality that we are to attribute to the whole company. About the chariot of Lygurge run great, white, muzzled hunting dogs, big as bullocks. Emetrius's pet animals are a white eagle, lions, and leopards. The fact that these animals are tame only makes the comparison with their masters the more impressive. And practically every other detail is a superlative, the quality of which contributes to martial or royal magnificence.

In some of the decriptions in the Knight's Tale, Chaucer is at his very best as a poet:

> The rede statue of Mars, with spere and targe,
> So shyneth in his white baner large,
> That alle the feeldes glyteren up and doun;
> And by his baner born in his penoun
> Of gold ful riche, in which ther was ybete
> The Mynotaur, which that he slough in Crete.
> Thus rit this duc, thus rit this conquerour,
> And in his hoost of chivalrie the flour.
>
> (l. 975ff.)

Even in so short a passage, the power bestowed on this description suggests a function deeper than mere ornament. It links with a score of other passages as an expression of Theseus's preeminence in war and chivalry. For instance the very opening of the poem, with its compressed but powerful description of the conquest of the Amazons and the marriage of Ypolita, is devoted to this end, and the texture of the following incident of the mourning women of Thebes, which acts as a kind of prologue to the Knight's Tale proper, widens and perpetuates our notion of Theseus as variously the ruler, the conqueror, the judge, and, not least, the man of pity. Among many subsequent details, the magnificence of the lists and of Arcite's funeral is directly associated with Theseus's dispensations.

The establishment of this preeminence is essential to the meaning of the poem and is carried out in many aspects of it. There is an obvious correspondence between the quality of these descriptions and the position of Theseus as the central figure in the poem's pattern of characters. And like the descriptions, the speeches in the poem have a great deal of metaphoric value. If they do not operate very effectively in the interest of plot and characterization—Theseus has been likened to Polonius!—it is because they serve other and more poetic ends; they too contribute to the pattern of tones and values which is the real substance of the poem. Those of Theseus again show him as representative of the highest chivalric conceptions of nobility. As the most noble human figure he presides over the events and interprets them. His final oration is a masterpiece of dignity. Theseus assembles his parliament, with Palamon and Emilye, to make an end of the mourning for Arcite. The speech is carefully and formally introduced:

> Whan they were set, and hust was al the place,
> And Theseus abiden hadde a space
> Er any word cam fram his wise brest,
> His eyen sette he ther as was his lest,
> And with a sad visage he siked stille,
> And after that right thus he seyde his wille.
>
> (l. 2981ff.)

The speech itself is adapted from Boethius. It is a monologue of *sentence* and doctrine in the medieval manner. The progress of it is logical and orderly: Theseus takes up first principles, then general examples from nature, and finally the matter in hand. Chaucer makes no effort to conceal its scholastic character. As a parliamentary address it is not outside the realm of possibility; but this is the least justification for it. A deeper one is its perfect agreement, in organization and content, with the principle of order which Theseus both invokes and represents throughout the tale. In a sense the representative of Fate on earth, the earthly sovereign interprets the will of the divine one:

> "Thanne may men by this ordre wel discerne
> That thilke Moevere stable is and eterne.
>
> (l. 3003f.)

> "What maketh this but Juppiter, the kyng,
> The which is prince and cause of alle thyng,
> Convertynge al unto his propre welle
> From which it is dirryved, sooth to telle?

> And heer-agayns no creature on lyve,
> Of no degree, availleth for to stryve.
> Thanne is it wysdom, as it thynketh me,
> To maken vertu of necessitee,
> And take it weel that we may nat eschue."
>
> (l. 3035ff.)

The king is an inveterate enemy to rebellion: "And whoso gruccheth ought, he dooth folye, / And rebel is to hym that al may gye" (ll. 3045–46). The principal representative of chivalry espouses a highly idealistic conception of the value of a good name:

> "And certainly a man hath moost honour
> To dyen in his excellence and flour,
> When he is siker of his goode name;
> Thanne hath he doon his freend, ne hym, no shame.
> And gladder oghte his freend been of his deeth,
> Whan with honour up yolden is his breeth,
> Than whan his name appalled is for age,
> For al forgeten is his vassellage.
> Thanne is it best, as for a worthy fame,
> To dyen whan that he is best of name."
>
> (l. 3047ff.)

The actions and speeches by the central figure are the normative ones in the poem. Those of Palamon and Arcite are lesser and contributory, in the sense that they only provide the questions and the elements of variety which are to be resolved; it is Theseus who expounds the resolutions. The knights' actions are, in fact, exemplary of life as it is lived. In this light, it is important to differentiate carefully between the balance of tone that Chaucer preserves in his treatment of them and the more or less direct evidences of satire and of tragedy which many critics have seemed to find there. Theseus's speech on the loves of Palamon and Arcite (ll. 1785–1820), for instance, has prompted the suggestion that here Chaucer revolts against the courtly code which the knights represent. First of all, it must be seen that the poet is not here dealing with courtly love per se, but only with love, on a par with chivalry, as one of the persistent facts of the noble life. The tournament is held, we remember, "For love and for encrees of chivalrye" (l. 2184). The emphasis, however, is not in the courtly allegory, where the inner life is explored and where the action revolves about the pursuit and defense of the lady's rose. The lady in the Knight's Tale is merely a symbol of the noble man's desires. And the question of love is never in debate here. We take love in this society for granted, and then go on to discover how faithfully experience in love exemplifies the partial blindness of all earthly experience. Love, we find, can create dissension between sworn brothers; can make a man lament his release from prison; make him forsake safety and native land; and, after unending toll of time and strength, it can leave him bloody and desirous of death. Theseus's speech on love, as his speech on Arcite's death, is normative and judicial; and to the noble, the mature mind, the paradoxically impractical quality of love is both laughable and admirable. The rivalry and consequent exploits of Palamon and Arcite are so impractical, and yet so much a reflex of their knightly spirits, that there is something to be said on both sides. Theseus's speech, therefore, is a mature appraisal, not an adverse criticism, of courtly love; certainly not a reflection of Chaucer's "strong revolt against the code."

The leavening, balancing element of common sense is signalized here, as it is usually signalized in Chaucer, by a lapse of the high style and the introduction of colloquialism:

> "But this is yet the beste game of alle,
> That she for whom they han this jolitee
> Kan hem therfore as muche thank as me.
> She woot namoore of al this hoote fare,
> By God, than woot a cokkow or an hare!"
>
> (l. 1806ff.)

With all this humorous ventilation of the subject, however, the real power of love is not denied:

> "But all moot ben assayed, hoot and coold;
> A man moot been a fool, or yong or oold,—
> I woot it by myself ful yore agon,
> For in my tyme a servant was I oon.
> And therfore, syn I knowe of loves peyne,
> And woot hou soore it kan a man distreyne,
> As he that hath ben caught ofte in his laas,
> I yow foryeve al hoolly this trespaas."
>
> (l. 1811ff.)

This kind of balance, if it precludes satire, does not of course rule out the possibility of irony. Indeed, such a tone is consonant with Theseus's maturity and dignity. But the several touches of this sort in the poem, and the tensions within its structure that might also be called ironic, neither point to the moral superiority of one knight nor support a tragic attitude toward either of them. It is true that, while Chaucer equalized the Palemone and Arcita of the *Teseida,* he carefully preserved a certain difference between them. One serves Venus, the other Mars. One prays for Emilye, the other for victory. But it does not appear that by preserving this distinction Chaucer implies any moral preference. As the whole background of the tale shows, the worship of Mars is no less important an aspect of the noble life than the worship of Venus. To Arcite go the honor in war, the magnificent funeral, and the intangible rewards brought out in Theseus's oration. To Palamon goes Emilye; in her are described the rewards that accrue to him as the servant of Venus. That the differentiation between the knights is ultimately a source of balance rather than of conflict can be seen even at the beginning of the poem. Palamon sees Emilye first, but his claim is balanced by Arcite's contention:

> "Thyn is affeccioun of hoolynesse,
> And myn is love, as to a creature."
> (l. 1158f.)

Now this distinction is not clearly carried out beyond the passage in question, although it has been expanded by critics to allegorical and morally significant proportions. And even if it did exist as a sustained and fundamental difference between the knights, it would not create a moral *issue* in the poem.

What further deadens any possibly moralistic or tragic implications in the fate of Arcite is a touch of Chaucer's lightness. Were Arcite's death ultimately attributable to some moral disjointedness of his own, we should expect it to be made abundantly clear. But in a literature in which the advent of death is one of the most powerful instruments of moral exemplum, Chaucer goes far out of his way to stifle any such construction. In describing Arcite's death, he involves the reader not in moral conclusions, but in complicated *physical* data with associations so cold and scientific that no moral conclusion can possibly be drawn (ll. 2743–58). The spirit of moral noncommitment is brought out clearly in the final lines of the narrator's comment, where again we see the leavening, common-sensical element expressed through colloquialism:

> Nature hath now no dominacioun.
> And certeinly, ther Nature wol nat wirche,
> Fare wel phisik! go ber the man to chirche!
> This al and som, that Arcita moot dye.
>
> (l. 2758ff.)

The critic must be on his guard here not to exaggerate the meaning of this digression, not to convert a deftly administered antidote for tragedy into an actively satiric strain. This would be to mistake Chaucer's balance for buffoonery. Immediately following this passage comes Arcite's most elevated speech. Were the narrator's remarks to be read as a satiric comment on Arcite's death, the whole noble fabric of the speech, and of the poem too, would crumble.

If Palamon and Arcite exemplify legitimate attitudes of equal value, and balance or supplement each other in providing not moral conflict but variety, we must look not at the relationship between them, but rather at their common position in relation to the universe, to find the real moral issue in the poem. And Chaucer expresses this issue not only through a tension between the poem's symmetrically ordered structure and the violent ups and downs of the surface narrative—too plainly to be seen to require elaborate analysis—but also through a complication of texture, in the weaving of darker threads among the red and gold.

I have already suggested that the poem's speeches, like its descriptions, are largely part of its texture; many of them are less important as pointing to specific psychological characteristics that issue in direct action than as elements in broader organizations, with deeper and more ulterior relevance to what goes on in the poem. Thus we have from Palamon and Arcite a considerable number of lyrics, some of them contributing only to the poem's general background of conventional love and chivalry, and others, more important, in which love lament melts into poetry of a more philosophical kind, and brings us to the heart of the issue. This latter characteristic of the poem's texture supports the view that love, which has been too often regarded as the poem's central theme, is used only as a vehicle of expression, a mode of experience of the noble life, which is itself the subject of the poem and the object of its philosophic questions. Thus, in the magnificent death speech of Arcite the lyric of love merges with the philosophical, the lady addressed becomes part of the speech's descriptive imagery, and the theme of love itself is subsumed in the category of all earthly experience:

> "Naught may the woful spirit in myn herte
> Declare o point of alle my sorwes smerte
> To yow, my lady, that I love moost;
> But I biquethe the servyce of my goost
> To yow aboven every creature,
> Syn that my lyf may no lenger dure.
> Allas, the wo! allas, the peynes stronge,
> That I for yow have suffred, and so longe!
> Allas, the deeth! allas, myn Emelye!
> Allas, departynge of oure compaignye!
> Allas, myn hertes queene! allas, my wyf!
> Myn hertes lady, endere of my lyf!
> What is this world? what asketh men to have?
> Now with his love, now in his colde grave
> Allone, withouten any compaignye."
>
> (l. 2765ff.)

Similarly, the speech of Arcite after his release from prison shifts from personal outcry to general speculation. Here, although Arcite mentions the paradoxical nature of men's designs with reference to the irony of his *own* position, he sounds a note which reechoes throughout the poem:

> "Som man desireth for to han richesse,
> That cause is of his mordre or greet siknesse;
> And som man wolde out of his prisoun fayn,
> That in his hous is of his meynee slayn."
>
> (l. 1255ff.)

The parallel lament of Palamon in prison is a variation on the same theme:

> "O crueel goddes that governe
> This world with byndyng of youre word eterne,
> And writen in the table of atthamaunt
> Youre parlement and youre eterne graunt,
> What is mankynde moore unto you holde

Than is the sheep that rouketh in the folde?
For slayn is man right as another beest,
And dwelleth eek in prison and arreest,
And hath siknesse and greet adversitee,
And ofte tymes giltelees, pardee.
What governance is in this prescience,
That giltelees tormenteth innocence?"
(l. 1303ff.)

The motive of misfortune and disorder is extended in ever-widening circles of reference in the descriptions of the three temples:

First in the temple of Venus maystow se
Wroght on the wal, ful pitous to biholde,
The broken slepes, and the sikes colde,
The sacred teeris, and the waymentynge,
The firy strokes of the desirynge
That loves servantz in this lyf enduren.
(l. 1918ff.)

On the walls of the temple of Diana are depicted the stories of Callisto, Daphne, Actaeon, and Meleager, all of unhappy memory. In the description of Mars's temple, the narrator is most powerful. He sees

the derke ymaginyng
Of Felonye, and al the compassyng;
The crueel Ire, reed as any gleede;
The pykepurs, and eek the pale Drede;
The smylere with the knyf under the cloke;
The shepne brennynge with the blake smoke;
The tresoun of the mordrynge in the bedde;
The open werre, with woundes al bibledde.
(l. 1995ff.)

In this context, the monologue of Saturn is the culminating expression of an ever-swelling undertheme of disaster:

"Myn is the drenchyng in the see so wan;
Myn is the prison in the derke cote;
Myn is the stranglyng and hangyng by the throte,
The murmure and the cherles rebellyng,
The groynynge, and the pryvee empoysonyng."
(l. 2456ff.)

In Theseus's majestic summary there is a final echo, the continuing rhetorical repetition as insistent as fate itself:

> "He moot be deed, the kyng as shal a page;
> Som in his bed, som in the depe see,
> Som in the large feeld, as men may see."
>
> (l. 3030ff.)

This subsurface insistence on disorder is the poem's crowning complexity, its most compelling claim to maturity. We have here no glittering, romantic fairy-castle world. The impressive, patterned edifice of the noble life, its dignity and richness, its regard for law and decorum, are all bulwarks against the ever-threatening forces of chaos, and in constant collision with them. And the crowning nobility, as expressed by this poem, goes beyond a grasp of the forms of social and civil order, beyond magnificence in any earthly sense, to a perception of the order beyond chaos. When the earthly designs suddenly crumble, true nobility is faith in the ultimate order of all things. Saturn, disorder, nothing more nor less, is the agent of Arcite's death, and Theseus, noble in the highest sense, interprets it in the deepest perspective. In contrast is the incomplete perception of the wailing women of Athens:

> "Why woldestow be deed," thise wommen crye,
> "And haddest gold ynough, and Emelye?"
>
> (l. 2835f.)

The history of Thebes had perpetual interest for Chaucer as an example of the struggle between noble designs and chaos. Palamon and Arcite, Thebans, lovers, fighters and sufferers, through whom the pursuit of the noble life is presented, exemplify through their experiences and express through their speeches this central conflict.

Keeping Appointments We Never Made

E. Talbot Donaldson

The Knight's Tale has been well described as a philosophical romance. Although the plot is derived from an epic, Giovanni Boccaccio's Italian poem *Il Teseida,* the tale's preoccupation with love and warfare is characteristic of the medieval chivalric romance. But the story's theme is perhaps of more significance than its form or plot. Palamon's success and Arcite's failure raise certain questions about the nature of the justice that disposes worldly events, and certain answers are suggested. The source for these is the sixth-century treatise *The Consolation of Philosophy* by the Roman philosophic writer Boethius. Boethian thought is, inevitably, somewhat modified by Chaucer in terms of the medieval chivalric ideal and of the prevailing pessimism of the late fourteenth century.

Boethius's book, one that appealed greatly to Chaucer, who translated it into English prose, was written when its author was in prison awaiting execution for crimes against the state. A man of much distinction as a public servant and a scholar, Boethius had become prominent in public affairs under the Visigothic Emperor Theodoric. But Boethius was a Roman of the classic mold, deeply concerned with preserving the traditional values of Roman government, and it was inevitable that his principles should bring him into collision with the far less scrupulous emperor. After a lifetime of service to Rome, Boethius found himself stripped of all honors and

From *Chaucer's Poetry: An Anthology for the Modern Reader,* edited by E. Talbot Donaldson. © 1958 by the Ronald Press Co.

condemned to death. The consolation that he proposed for this sad predicament takes the form of a dialogue between himself and Philosophy, personified as a woman who visits him in his prison. Finding him lamenting his fate and abusing Fortune, Philosophy gradually persuades him to assume philosophical equanimity, so that by the end of the dialogue Boethius understands the nature of the world well enough to become reconciled with his lot. The book amounts, on the practical level, to a demonstration of the principle that the man who devotes himself to the values of the spirit may remain unmoved by whatever ill fortune befalls him. According to Philosophy, the world is governed, if remotely, by a deity who represents the highest good: that there is a divine plan is evident to the philosopher, even if he cannot understand the details of it. But by having confidence in its existence and by valuing only what is really good in this world—that is, what at least partakes of the highest good—a man may achieve a state of mind in which external evil is reduced to an irrelevant illusion, even the evil that befalls him. Though Boethius was a Christian and his book relies on Christian ethics, he makes no specific reference to Christianity and by avoiding the issue of the life to come places the emphasis of his thought on this world and man's deportment in it—precisely what Chaucer does in the Knight's Tale. It is this emphasis that makes Boethius's book and Chaucer's tale both so strongly stoic: with no promise of reward or punishment man must adjust himself to life on earth as if there were no other. If one finds it surprising that the intensely Christian Chaucer, writing in the intensely Christian Middle Ages, should in a serious philosophic poem eschew the Christian solution to the problem of earthly justice, one must bear in mind that Boethius's book, which made the same eschewal, was very popular with the Middle Ages in general.

In the Knight's Tale the philosophic problem is why of two young men equally worthy (or unworthy) one should live to attain happiness with the woman he loves and the other should end, through the most capricious of accidents, in his grave, "allone, withouten any compaignye." The answer given by Theseus, who is the spokesman for the poem's overt philosophy, is simply that there is no reason that man can hope to understand. Nevertheless, behind all apparent accidents it is necessary to believe that there lies the will of a benevolent deity who resides at the center of the great universe in which our world is but a remote point. And far removed as it is, our world is still controlled by the great chain that proceeds from the Prime Mover. Since man cannot know the Prime Mover's purposes, he must accept willingly what comes to him—and, in practical terms, "make a virtue of necessity." The poem's emphasis on necessity results in a statement that is rather less consoling than Boethius's: fate seems to operate with a petty malignancy to frustrate to the last detail the wills of the characters, and its predominating part in everyday life becomes—as it is intended to be—oppressive. This oppressiveness undoubtedly reflects the increasing pessimism of the later Middle Ages. On the other hand, while the poem's picture of life is a dreary one in many ways, there is no tendency within it to urge on the reader the ascetic escape from life that frequently is associated with the stoic attitude. The characters are enjoined—as Theseus enjoins Palamon and Emily—to live life as fully and as richly as destiny will permit: if Arcite's death is seemingly senseless and unjust, it at least enables him to die with his glory untarnished—and it enables Palamon to have his desire at long last. There is a practical economy about this attitude that is both Chaucerian and also characteristic of his simultaneously pessimistic and pleasure-loving era. And in the paradoxical attitude that Theseus sets forth, that man ought to maintain a suspicious and detached attitude toward a world in which he must be wholeheartedly involved, there is something peculiarly Chaucerian.

One naturally responds to a rivalry such as that between Palamon and Arcite by taking sides. Some critics have argued that Palamon is the worthier of the two; but others have sided with Arcite, considering him the more deserving. Chaucer probably expected the reader to take sides, but if he intended that one young man should be recognized as the worthier he seems to have gone about it badly. The claims of the two are equally balanced: in any one scene Palamon may be more admirable than Arcite, but in the next Arcite will behave better than Palamon. Neither of them behaves consistently better than the other up to Arcite's death, the nobility of which should cancel any doubts about Arcite's essential worthiness, just as Palamon's sincere grief at Arcite's death should cancel any doubts about Palamon's worthiness. The truth seems to be that the young men are on an even footing and that, from the earthly point of view, justice operates with equal whimsicality in bringing Arcite to death and Palamon to happiness. This is what the overt theme of the tale, presented by Theseus, makes clear.

On the other hand, it must be remembered that justice merely seems whimsical to dwellers on earth, while the divine plan must be just; and something of this higher justice appears within the poem to lend support to Theseus's postulation of the divine plan. It is undeniably fitting that Palamon, who initially mistook Emily for Venus, who dedicates himself as Venus's knight, and who prays not for victory but for Emily, should in the end get the heroine; it is equally fitting that Arcite, who worships Mars and asks for victory, should win the tournament. But on the moral plane the issues are unresolved and remain as curiously remote as the divine plan itself. It is difficult to find in Venus and Mars satisfactory allegories of the moral characters of Palamon and Arcite, as some have tried to do. Chaucer has been at pains to show Venus's temple as little more cheerful a place than Mars's; and in the effective astrological action, lest the planetary attributes of beneficent Venus should seem to symbolize the moral superiority of her knight over the servant of the maleficent Mars, Chaucer replaces Venus by the most baleful of all the planets, Saturn, and he is the direct agent of Palamon's eventual victory. Besides, one must remember that chivalry was equally a matter of love and warfare, of Venus and Mars, and a knight whose moral conduct was all Venerean or all Martian was only half a knight. In their actions Palamon and Arcite are equally the warrior and the lover. Therefore the rightness of Venus's eventual victory cannot be extended to Palamon's character; rather, it reflects a supramoral perception of the way the universe is conducted.

The tale does not show Chaucer as particularly interested in the characterization of individuals. The heroine Emily is a symbol of the loveliness life and society have to offer, but her effect is generalized: she is beautiful, therefore lovable. Palamon and Arcite are differentiated in individual scenes, but neither stands out especially from the generality of brave, lovestruck young men. Perhaps the most memorable character is Theseus, who gives the poem's theme overt expression and whose own actions are a demonstration of the stoicism which never ceases to struggle with a bad world. He sees that the world is chaotic, but with his every considered action he tries to bring to this chaos as much order as he can. Like the Almighty, his first consideration is always the imposition of order: he interrupts his homecoming in order to avenge Creon's insults to the widowed queens; he ordains that the young knights will fight it out in the lists rather than in the woods; he builds the lists in a splendidly formal fashion; he arranges the magnificent funeral for Arcite; and he, in the end, joins Palamon and Emily. That the bringing of order involves cruelty—the destruction of Thebes, the imprisonment of the heroes, even their execution—represents the practical compromise that, moral or not, medieval chivalry believed in. So chaotic a world could never be returned to a prelapsarian state. To make it livable at all the ruler could not, it was thought, be forgiving to the point of softness. Medieval chivalry would have accepted the execution of Palamon and Arcite that Theseus first ordains as something right and proper—though it was capable also of accepting the mercy the women beg him to grant as something better.

Aside from its chivalric plot, the Knight's Tale is admirably suited to its narrator, whose personality, not much revealed in the idealism of the portrait in the General Prologue, is allowed to develop within the bounds of the same idealism. Against the excesses of the plot the Knight's firm self-control is constantly reflected. He has—like Theseus—sympathy with the rash young men and their foolish actions while he recognizes their rashness and folly for what they are. At every point in the story where emotion tends to become swollen and disorderly he is quick to restrain it. For he seems to recognize and practice a principle that is a part of the Boethian system but was not much practiced by the Middle Ages, as it is not always practiced by the hotheaded Theseus—namely, that excessive emotion is an enslavement of the spirit and a threat to order. At several of the most serious moments of the poem, the Knight's humor provides an antidote to the overinvolvement of the characters in their fate. He is, after all, an old soldier who has observed that deaths in battle have no connection with any recognizable system of earthly justice and that to expect a good man to avoid an ill end is to expose oneself to paralyzing frustration. It is necessary to go on living in this uncertain world, doing the best one can, always expecting the worst to happen. As he himself puts it,

> It is ful fair a man to bere him evene,
> For alday meeteth men at unset stevene.

"It is a good thing for a man to bear himself with equanimity, for one is constantly keeping appointments one never made." Or, as Shakespeare was later to say, "The readiness is all."

The Meaning of Chaucer's Knight's Tale

Douglas Brooks and Alastair Fowler

The critical problem presented by the Knight's Tale is still the simple primary one of interpretation. What is the tale about? Most readers and critics agree that it cannot be regarded as a simple external narrative, after the manner of much of Boccaccio's *Teseida*. Its psychology seems too debatable for that, its descriptive passages too powerful and richly symbolic. Yet the difficulties of deciding what forms of organization Chaucer has added—whether philosophical, moral, or psychological—have proved formidable. Indeed, one of the best of the poem's critics, Charles Muscatine, has been provoked into cutting the gordian knot by asking the more radical question, Is the tale about anything? And he gives the answer that "the Knight's Tale is essentially neither a story, nor a static picture, but a poetic pageant, and that all its materials are organized and contributory to a complex design expressing the nature of the noble life." While admiring Muscatine's sure sense of the tale's ceremonial gravity and nobility, we cannot rest content with a description that would apply equally well to so many other literary works. The description is hard to quarrel with, but only because it is too broad to have a disprovable content. Every romance expresses the nature of the noble life. Besides, the detachment of texture from subject postulated by Muscatine is altogether too Mannerist to be possible at this date. We may reasonably expect an early Renaissance narrative work, and specifically a work of Chaucer's, to have subject, theme and story, and a poetic impact

From *Medium Aevum* 39, no. 2 (1970). © 1970 by the Society for the Study of Mediaeval Languages and Literature.

closely related to these elements. This is so with the other *Canter-bury Tales* and it is so with the Knight's Tale.

The primary problem of interpretation presents itself in practice as three specific difficulties in reading the poem. First, seeing the meaning and full relevance to the human action of the mythological episodes (ll. 2438–78, 2663–70). The problem here is not rendered any the less acute by our knowledge that these passages are largely original with Chaucer. Secondly, seeing the relevance of the elaborate description of the champion kings Lygurge and Emetreus, who support Palamon and Arcite in the tournament. True, W. C. Curry has shown that the champion kings have pronounced physiognomical characteristics, such as would be produced by the influence of the two maleficent planetary deities. But to say that Lygurge is Saturnian and Emetreus Martian does not apparently help our understanding of the tale as a whole. And, indeed, Muscatine, in desperation, falls back on a simpler consensus view: for him the "contribution to the surface narrative" of the portraits of Emetreus and Lygurge is "slight"—"the imagery is organized around no central conception of personality, but rather connotes the magnificence that befits nobility."

Thirdly, and most crucially, there is the difficulty of distinguishing between Palamon and Arcite, who seem so alike in terms of ordinary moral and psychological characterization. H. N. Fairchild's schematic contrast between a contemplative Palamon and an active Arcite has not met with much acceptance. In fact some critics, taking advantage of the slenderness of naturalistic characterization, have actually stood Fairchild's evaluation on its head and defended Arcite. J. R. Hulbert, however, finds the poem defective in character altogether: he sees it as posing a courtly *demande d'amour* such as no modern reader can take seriously. Who cares which hero wins Emelye? Subsequent criticism, though taking the tale more seriously, has in different ways minimized its heroes' moral and psychological differences. Muscatine goes so far as to hail "the equalization of Palamon and Arcite" as Chaucer's "crowning modification" of the *Teseida,* allowing a formal symmetry that he regards as the English poem's principal source of satisfaction. Even D. W. Robertson's *A Preface to Chaucer,* generally eager to restore the moral and theological significances of which previous criticism emptied Chaucer's poetry, makes no distinction between Palamon and Arcite, except a little in the extent of their corruption: Arcite suffers from the disease of love and its consequent "manye," while "Palamon's condition differs only in degree," so that the tale offers no subject for dramatic identification. But we may suppose that, if Palamon and Arcite were always indistinguishable, the tale must have been unsatisfactory and puzzling to its first readers too.

Yet the Knight's Tale remains a good, perhaps a great, poem. Can a literary work whose intention is so doubtful deserve such an estimate? Only if the import and meaning were formerly clearer—potentially, at least—than they have since become. It need not follow that the clearer meaning is recoverable. *Volat irrevocabile*. But in this case, fortunately, Chaucer's consistency, unity, even clarity, can be vindicated. From an examination of descriptive details (more often significant than not, in his work) underlying schemes of thought once taken for granted but now obscure can be reconstructed. In relation to these reconstructed schemes the particular problems mentioned above are resolved and the different parts of the poem seen to be meaningfully articulated. We propose a new interpretation starting from two assumptions: first, that Chaucer's poem is organized in the early Renaissance manner, with details belonging harmoniously to an overall simple unity of meaning and form; secondly, that Curry's work on the champion kings carries an ineluctable implication—the tale's psychological content must be expressed through emblematic symbolism rather than naturalistic characterization.

II

The bearing of the mythological episode depends on a system of correspondences between the tale's planetary deities and human characters. Chaucer's point is that these deities do not merely influence human affairs sporadically or at random: they have each constant protégés under their special patronage. The decorative programmes of the three temples at the lists draw attention to this in a very direct way, in fact, for in each Chaucer has made use of the familiar convention whereby a planetary deity's influence was shown by portraying a group of his "children"—that is, those carrying on the trades, professions and activities under his patronage. And when, in the same temples, the two lovers and their lady make their critical intercessions on the morning of the tournament, each displays a devotion too intimate to be a matter of casual whim.

The correspondence most obvious in its main lines, yet also the most complex, is that between Jupiter and Theseus. Theseus, "lord and governour" of Athens, throughout the tale dominates the political order, manifesting in turn the qualities of a just ruler and a wise king, as the Knight conceives them. Thus he displays the imperial virtue *Clementia* when he is moved to take pity on the wronged widows who waylay him at the "temple of the goddesse Clemence" (l. 928, F. N. Robinson, 2d ed.), and when he revenges them he displays the complementary virtue of *Iustitia*. Later, in parting Palamon and Arcite, and again at the tournament, Theseus assumes the role of arbiter: "I wol be trewe juge" (l. 2657). In all these respects he shows himself the child of Jupiter:

> In his magisterial capacity Jupiter possesses adequate knowledge pertaining to law, delivers just decisions, and judges with integrity. When he beholds men engaged in altercations and litigations, he has the happy faculty of restoring peace and establishing concord among them.
>
> (Alcabitius)

For Jupiter is governor of the gods, *necessitas,* the ultimate power—as indeed Theseus himself pronounces at the climax of the poem: "What maketh this but Juppiter, the kyng, / That is prince and cause of alle thyng?" (l. 3035f.).

Nevertheless, additional planetary influences are clearly at work in Theseus's character. The activity of the moment might adequately account for the Knight's statement that "after Mars he serveth now Dyane" (l. 1682). But he rode against Creon under a banner specifically charged with the image of Mars (ll. 975–77). And an emotional disposition is unambiguously indicated when Theseus interrupts the forest duel of Palamon and Arcite, trembling with rage and threatening them with death, in speeches that begin and end with invocations of Mars:

> "By myghty Mars, he shal anon be deed."
>
> (l. 1708)

> "Ye shal be deed, by myghty Mars the rede!"
>
> (l. 1747)

Again he is moved to pity, however, by a company of weeping ladies. Mars is tempered by Venus, so that Theseus not only spares the two lovers but exclaims at the power of love:

> "The god of love, a, *benedicite!*
> How myghty and how greet a lord is he!"
>
> (l. 1785f.)

Appreciation of this incident partly depends on a knowledge of the mediating function of Jupiter. Like Luna, Jupiter was a temperate deity, who held extremes in concord. In particular, he was supposed to mediate judiciously between rough Mars and soft Venus. The acknowledgment of love's power quoted above, coming so soon after oaths by Mars, may be seen as Theseus's binding of Mars by Cupid. Earlier, the same child of Jupiter, who knew by experience "of loves peyne" (l. 1815) united Mars and Venus—though as martially as possible—in his marriage with the Amazonian queen Ypolita.

Considered in this light, Theseus might appear the ideal arbiter between Palamon and Arcite. And so, for a time, until the tournament itself, things seem to work out. But—and this is one of the tale's difficulties—it is ultimately not Theseus who resolves the conflict between Palamon and Arcite, just as in the heavens it is not Jupiter who resolves the conflict "Bitwixe Venus, the goddesse of love, / And Mars, the stierne god armypotente" (l. 2440f.). Jupiter is "bisy" to stop that strife, but ineffectually: somewhat surprisingly it is "pale Saturnus the colde" who, against his nature (l. 2451) "gan remedie fynde"—a remedy capable of answering everyone's prayer. And on earth as in heaven Jupiter's authority is again undercut by Saturn: Theseus may declare, "I wol be trewe juge, and no partie. / Arcite of Thebes shal have Emelie" (l. 2657f.). But he awards victory only to see it snatched away by the god whose course has more power than any man knows (l. 2455): Arcite is thrown from his horse through the agency of a fury "sent at request of Saturne" (l. 2685).

Saturn, like Jupiter, has his earthly counterpart, this time in Egeus. Egeus is Theseus's "olde fader" (l. 2838), just as Saturn is mythologically father of Jupiter. And it is he whose counsel brings the human action to a resolution, corresponding to the heavenly accord reached by following the advice of Saturn. The main basis of correspondence lies in the fact that Saturn is the god of old age, the age of wisdom. Thus the line in the mythological episode, describing Saturn, "In elde is bothe wysdom and usage" (l. 2448), is complemented by the description of Egeus exhorting the people "ful wisely" (l. 2851). Indeed, Egeus's sole function seems to be to instruct Theseus when he is at a loss, helplessly grieving over the death of the victorious Arcite. Egeus's qualification for this role of comforter is his knowledge of "this worldes transmutacioun": "he hadde seyn it chaunge bothe up and doun" (l. 2839f.). The child of Saturn, god of time, is naturally an expert on mutability.

Emelye's mythological connections are in some ways the most instructive of all from the point of view of the present enquiry. Primarily, she is a child of Diana-Luna. For this correspondence we have the explicit evidence of her devotions before the tournament. It is to Diana's temple that she goes, to pray to the goddess of "thre formes" (l. 2313), Luna-Diana-Proserpina. There Emelye prays that the Martian Arcite and the Venerean Palamon may be reconciled: "sende love and pees bitwixe hem two" (l. 2317). She hopes that this may be achieved through her own virginity—that is, through the mediating influence of Luna as she understands it. Consequently she prays that Palamon's and Arcite's love may be quenched or turned from her (ll. 2318–21):

> "Syn thou art mayde and kepere of us alle,
> My maydenhede thou kepe and wel conserve,
> And whil I lyve, a mayde I wol thee serve."
>
> (ll. 2328–30)

At the same time, there are also hints of Venus in the portrayal of Emelye. Indeed, when she is first introduced, Palamon actually takes her for the goddess, or at least her transfigured appearance: "I noot wher she be womman or goddesse, / But Venus is it soothly, as I gesse" (l. 1101f.). More obliquely, one of Emelye's characteristic actions conceals an astronomical symbolism that carries the same implication. It was her habit to rise with the sun, or even "er it were day" (l. 1040ff., cf. l. 2273): an allusion, clearly, to the astronomical Venus, the morning star. The mingling of these two contrasting deities in Emelye should not, however, surprise us, for the tale is moving here towards the familiar Renaissance composite figure Venus-Diana, symbolic of the moral ideal of virtuous love. (Significantly, Emelye's "yelow heer"—a colour of Venus's—was carefully "broyded in a tresse.") These features of Emelye are only present, of course, in potentia; but they help us to understand her experience at the temple of Diana, when she discovers the threefold goddess to be more mysterious than she had realized.

Already in the description of Diana's temple, the goddess has been depicted not only as chaste huntress but also as Proserpina, wife of Pluto, and as Lucina, patroness of women in childbirth (ll. 2081–87): now, in the incident of Emelye's prayer, virginity is again shown to be only one of the stages of female life over which the goddess presides. The incident, in fact, is best approached as psychological allegory. Emelye is afraid to enter on the next stage of life, marriage, with all that signifies, so that her first prayer is an outright expression of her desire to remain virgin: "Chaste goddesse, wel wostow that I / Desire to ben a mayden al my lyf" (l. 2304f.). At the same time she recognizes the possible inappropriateness of this attitude—"if my destynee be shapen so / That I shal nedes have oon of hem two" (l. 2323f.)—and is drawn forward by a natural interest in the opposite sex. Amusingly enough (and in this we can hear the Knight's irony) Emelye finds herself praying to Diana of all goddesses to "sende me hym that moost desireth me" (l. 2325). The answering omen of the quenched altar fire is decisive. For the blazing brand is an attribute of Venus and Hymen, while the blood dripping from it represents the blood shed in menstruation, defloration and childbirth. At first Emelye is terrified, not knowing what the omen signifies (l. 2343). But then she learns that it means marriage: "Thou shalt ben wedded" (l. 2351). In other words, to put it in paler and more prosaic terms, Emelye must grow up and accept the onset of the next stage of her maturity. She has to pass from the patronage of Diana to that of Venus, and learn Venus's ways, just as Theseus has to be instructed in the ways of Saturn. The point is neatly, if unobtrusively, expressed in l. 2486f. ("al that Monday justen they and daunce, / And spenden it in Venus heigh servyse") for, in the planetary week, Monday is dedicated to Luna, so that here Luna has surrendered her day to Venus.

The correspondences with Palamon and Arcite at first sight seem simpler, in that they are more broadly and explicitly drawn. In the strife among the gods Venus takes Palamon's part and Mars Arcite's, in response, obviously, to the mortals' prayers. And these prayers may be expected to be in decorum with the nature of the worshippers. Arcite prays to Mars because he is a child of Mars, Palamon to Venus because he is a child of Venus—her "owene knyght" (l. 2471), in fact, to use Saturn's words. This has still to be demonstrated in terms of moral character, but it is already clear that all the actions of the lovers, at the time of the tournament that sums up their opposition, are performed in accordance with the appropriate planetary influence. Thus, as W. C. Curry has shown, each lover (and also Emelye) goes to pray at the hour of the astrological week presided over by the deity addressed. Moreover, the tournament that gives Arcite victory significantly takes place on the Tuesday, *dies Martis*—though the victor will be thrown from his horse at one of the hours of that day presided over by Saturn.

To these decorums may be added a further harmony, which

expresses even more fully the interrelation of planetary influences and human actions. For it appears that the architectural design of the lists, even the physical arrangement of the characters at the beginning of the tournament, is subject to a formal organization that has its astrological meaning. Everyone who reads the Knight's Tale is struck by the elaborate extensiveness of the descriptions of the lists and of the oratories prepared by Theseus during the year (l. 1850) that elapses between Palamon's and Arcite's first duel and their second. Much of the tale's third part, indeed, is occupied by these descriptions. Yet their relevance is no longer understood. The account of the design of the lists—"Round was the shap, in manners of compas, / Ful of degrees" (l. 1889f.)—leaves no doubt that a mathematical construction is intended. In one sense, of course, the *degrees* are simply the graduated levels on which spectators will be set (l. 1891); but we are also told that the design occupied the attention of every available "crafty man / That geometrie or arsmetrike kan" (l. 1897f.). What can this round construction be, with its carefully calculated positions for domiciles of planetary deities? Only a zodiac. The Knight's statement that "swich a place / Was noon in erthe" (l. 1895f.) has a special sense for the reader that it did not have for the pilgrims. It hints that the lists are a cosmic model. In confirmation of this is the vast size of the lists—a mile in circumference.

The siting of all the domiciles or temples to Mars, Venus and Diana, moreover, is in accordance with an actual state of the heavens. It will be recalled that Palamon and Arcite fought their first duel on Saturday May 5 and that Theseus instructed them to return a year later for the tournament. This instruction they obeyed to the letter, arriving at Athens on Sunday May 5 of the following year (l. 2188). Sunday night and early Monday morning were given over to the devotions of Palamon, Emelye and Arcite, and Monday May 6 was a feast day, spent in Venus's service (l. 2189), so that the tournament itself took place on Tuesday May 7. On that day, before the sun had fully risen—"It nas nat of the day yet fully pryme" (l. 2576)—Theseus and the spectators took their places "in degrees about" and Arcite entered "westward, thurgh the gates under Marte" (l. 2581), that is, under the house of Mars situated above the western gate:

> And in that selve moment Palamon
> Is under Venus, estward in the place.
>
> (l. 2584f.)

Now at sunrise on May 7 in the late fourteenth century the sign on the eastern horizon was Taurus, a domicile of Venus, while the sign on the western horizon was Scorpio, a domicile of Mars. Cancer, the only domicile of Luna, lay on the north-drawn meridian—where the oratory of Diana was situated, in fact, "northward in a touret on the wal." As for Theseus, "set . . . ful riche and hye" (l. 2577), his position seems to correspond to midheaven, where indeed we should expect to find one "arrayed right as he were a god in trone," in the seat of cosmic judgment. Here, however, there is a subtlety. For on May 7 there culminated, not the domicile of Jupiter we expect, but Capricorn, a domicile of Saturn:

Medium coeli

CAPRICORN:
domicile
of Saturn

TAURUS:		SCORPIO:
E. domicile		domicile W.
of Venus:		of Mars:
Palamon		Arcite

CANCER:
domicile
of Luna

Imum Coeli

N.

Yet again, it seems, the authority of Theseus and Jupiter has been undercut by Saturn.

Our examination of the correspondence between the planetary deities and their protégés has, then, served to integrate the mythological digression with the rest of the tale, and to show that the mythological and human actions are closely interrelated. But we are left more curious than ever as to what the import of all these planetary influences may be. And our difficulty with respect to the assistant kings has if anything been increased.

III

To support Palamon in the tournament comes Lygurge, king of Thrace; to support Arcite, Emetreus, king of India. The arrivals of the assistant kings are elaborately described in two immediately succeeding passages in part 3, which are obviously carefully balanced against one another (ll. 2128–54, 2155–86). But the problem is to see how the kings are related to their respective knights. Curry, the only critic to attempt a solution, has analysed the descriptions of the kings from a physiognomic point of view. He finds that "Emetreus, who comes to support Arcite the protégé of Mars, is a typical Martian figure; and Lycurgus, who aids Palamon, now under the protection of Saturn, is Saturnalian in form." Some of the details of Curry's argument are convincing, but his general conclusion creates far more problems than it solves. In particular, his offhand description of Palamon as "now under the protection of Saturn" begs a large question. Why is not Lygurge Venerean, as the simple symmetry of the tournament seems to require? Why is the contest not the direct "strif" between Mars and Venus that it appears to be in heaven? Alternatively, if we accept the association of Lygurge with Saturn, why should that planetary deity contend with Mars, when he means to give him the interim victory in any case? What can it possibly mean that the two unfortunate planets should contend? Such a conflict seems, indeed, to make astrological nonsense.

Answers to these questions can be given—but only after the iconology of the descriptions of Lygurge and Emetreus has been analysed more closely. We begin by adducing further evidence to confirm the surprising identification of Lygurge, Palamon's ally, as a child of Saturn. As Curry has shown, Lygurge's physical appearance marks him out physiognomically as Saturnian. The black beard (l. 2130), the "kempe heeris" (l. 2134), the "lymes grete" (l. 2135): all these details carry the same implication. Going beyond physiognomy, we note that Lygurge, "grete kyng of Trace" (l. 2129), is modelled on the Thracian king Lycurgus of ancient myth, who fought against Bacchus-Dionysus on his return from India: that Dionysus's Thracian war was against Saturn would be sufficient authority for making Lygurge Saturnian. In addition, the associations of all the animals in the description, both those mentioned as present and those appearing only as images, have a similar parameter. Thus Saturn's chariot, like Lygurge's (l. 2139), was drawn by bulls, in accordance with the extreme slowness of his orbit. Obviously, Lygurge could not simultaneously have his chariot drawn by the alternative griffins, but he could himself be described as looking "like a grifphon." Similarly, his hair (l. 2144) is as black as the raven, a bird often associated with *Tristitia* or Melancholy. And the huge dogs that surround his chariot (l. 2148) were familiar symbols of the same temperament.

Other particulars of the description seem to have a moral rather than a psychological meaning. It is noteworthy, for example, that whereas Emetreus rides on a horse, Lygurge stands on "a chaar of gold" (l. 2138). The primary reference here is of course to the Saturnian *aurea aetas;* but there may also be an allusion to Saturn's gift of Prudence, the "charioteer of the virtues." In schemes associating the seven gifts of the Holy Spirit with the seven planets, the supreme gift—Prudence or Wisdom—was most often allotted to Saturn, the planet of outermost orbit. Equally striking is the prominence of gold in the equipment of Lygurge's entourage. His chariot is of gold, his dogs' muzzles are "colored of gold" (l. 2152) and the nails of his bearskin are "yelewe and brighte as any gold" (l. 2141). Gold was sometimes in itself attributed to Saturn, because of its weight. But gold *muzzles* suggests more specifically the gold of restraint, and the gold nails of the bear confirm this connection, since the bear could apparently be an emblem of "Perfection with age and discipline." A similar but more obvious train of thought emphasizes instead the fact that the bear has been skinned and therefore killed: traditionally the bear was associated with anger and the choleric temperament, so that the details seem to mean that Lygurge has overcome the bear of anger. A closely related implication is probably to be seen in the "wrethe of gold, arm-greet, of huge wighte . . . set ful of stones brighte, / Of fyne rubyes and of dyamauntz" (ll. 2145–47), since the gold wreath in itself was a symbol of reward for virtue. But the diamond and ruby are Martian-Solar, and hence associated with the choleric temperament, so that the appropriation of the jewels parallels exactly the killing of the bear. At the same time, there may also be a suggestion that Saturn's course is "so wyde for to turne" (l. 2454) that it contains in its circle the powers of the lower planets.

Emetreus responds equally well to iconological analysis, though in this case the result does not altogether bear out Curry's conclusion. Emetreus's Martian qualities, it is true, are immediately apparent. On a bay steed with steel trappings he "Cam ridynge lyk the god of armes, Mars" (l. 2159). As Curry points out, the "eyen bright citryn" (l. 2167), the "sangwyn" colour and the "frakenes" or freckles (l. 2169) were all Martian attributes. To complement Lygurge's Saturnian menagerie, moreover, Emetreus has one that, in part at least, is Martian. He carries a Martian eagle, is accompanied by Martian leopards and rides a Martian horse of Martian colour. He himself speaks with a martial voice like "a trompe thonderynge" (l. 2174). Even his age, twenty-five, alludes to a number dedicated to Mars.

Nevertheless Emetreus is not to be explained simply as a child of Mars. Indeed, Solar attributes and Solar imagery are almost equally prominent in his description. Physiognomically, this is made quite explicit: "His crispe heer lyk rynges was yronne, / And that was yelow, and glytered as the sonne" (l. 2165f.). We need not try, as Curry does, to force this detail into the Martian mould. Chaucer says sun and means it. As for the description of Emetreus's facial complexion—

> his colour was sangwyn;
> A fewe frakenes in his face yspreynd,
> Bitwixen yelow and somdel blak ymeynd
> (ll. 2168–70)

—it seems to apply equally well to Solar and Martian subjects. Thus Agrippa of Nettesheim tells us that "the *Sun* makes a man of a tauny colour, betwixt yellow and black, dasht with red."

Other details of the description are either exclusively Solar, or ambiguous in their associations between Solar and Martian. The lions that surrounded Emetreus (l. 2185ff.) and that he himself is compared to (l. 2171) are in terms of planetary associations obstinately Solar—though they might indicate wrath and the choleric temperament. The leopards, which, as we have seen, were Martian, may also have been known to Chaucer as attributes of Dionysus, the winter sun. The eagle, as a primate, was often associated with Sol the sovereign planet. Even the horse has to be distinguished as Martian by its colour, because the horse in itself was often a Solar attribute. In the same way, the "laurer grene . . . gerland" (l. 2175ff.) worn by Emetreus is a Martian crown of victory, but made from a Solar plant. The gold of his saddle and trappings, however, like the rubies sparkling on his mantle, are in this context simply Solar; while the "perles white and rounde and grete" (l. 2161) with which his coat armour is couched are an association with India, the place Emetreus and Dionysus alike left for their wars with Lycurgus and Saturn.

It should be stressed that Emetreus's Martian and Solar qualities are in no way antithetic. On the contrary, they complement each other, since the two planets were regarded as being very similar in character. Mars was "hot and dry, cholerick and fiery": Sol was "Hot, Dry" and had "dominion of fire and cleere shining flames." Throughout the description of Emetreus, indeed—as was the case, we now see, with Lygurge too—the emphasis is more on the nature and attributes of a complexion than on those of a planetary influence. The introduction of the second planetary deity Sol, otherwise confusing, puts this beyond doubt. There will be no confusion if the details, both Martian and Solar, are regarded as symbols of the choleric complexion. Thus the rubies of Emetreus's mantlet are "rede as fyr" (l. 2164), the corresponding element. His lions were attributes of Mars because they were first choleric animals. And in an engraving by Virgil Solis the choleric complexion is represented, as here, by lion and eagle together. It goes without saying that Emetreus's lions are tame because they are in accord with his complexion, while Lygurge, by contrast, hunts lions with his huge dogs, just as he hunted the bear to acquire the skin he wears. Choleric bears and lions are to him not tame attributes, but wild animals to be conquered in the hunt, symbol of life's arduous moral pursuit.

Although this enquiry has clarified the function of many descriptive details, it does not at first seem to have taken us very far beyond Curry's position. We know that the opposition of Lygurge and Emetreus is not an opposition of Saturnian and Martian influences, but of Saturnian and Martian-Solar influences; or, rather, of melancholic and choleric complexions. But we are still faced with the question what such an opposition can mean. We believe that the answer lies in the indications of age that are included in both descriptions—Lygurge's face "manly" (l. 2130) and bearded, his bearskin black "for old" (l. 2142), Emetreus's appearance of being "of fyve and twenty yeer" (l. 2172) with a beard "wel bigonne for to sprynge" (l. 2173). For these details, taken together with the attributes of planetary deities and complexions, would bring to the mind of any mediæval reader the familiar scheme of the Four Ages of Man. In that scheme, planetary influences, complexions and ages were correlated as in the accompanying Table:

AGE	PLANET	ELEMENT	COMPLEXION
I Youth (0–20)	Jupiter (and Venus)	Air	Sanguinic
II Prime (20–40)	Mars	Fire	Choleric
III Middle Age (40–60)	Saturn	Earth	Melancholic
IV Old Age (60–)	Moon (and Venus)	Water	Phlegmatic

Lygurge is clearly a representative of the Third Age, just as Emetreus is of the Second. Moreover, as the Ages are portrayed in the tale (though this was by no means generally the case) the sequence from Age II to Age III is a moral sequence. Lygurge, that is to say, is in the fullest sense more mature than Emetreus. He hunts choleric animals, he can assimilate the choleric virtues symbolized in his diamond-and-ruby wreath, because he had left behind the fiery impetuosity of youth. Through the temperance and restraint appropriate to his age and manifested, as we have seen, in his emblematic accoutrements, he has matured to a stage of experience beyond that of Arcite's Dionysiac ally. The Lycurgus of ancient legend, we recall, was a lawgiver. It is in keeping with this polarity that Lygurge should wear the jewelled wreath that symbolized the rewards of virtue, and Emetreus merely the laurel wreath of victory.

We would not be thought to imply that the assistant kings' poetic function and meaning can be exhausted solely in terms of the theme of the Ages of Man. They have a part also in the narrative and emotional movement of the third part of the tale. Thus, they arrive between the static descriptions of the temples of the planetary deities, decorated with murals showing their fixed influence on human activities (ll. 1893–2088), and the narrative of prayers to living and responding gods (ll. 2209–2437). Their advent is, in fact, Palamon's and Arcite's summoning up of their deepest psychological resources. The terms of life's contest have already been fixed in imagery strange and dark enough, but the arrival of the kings is told in a passage even stranger: an appropriate bridge to the religious experiences to follow. Indeed, the kings' entourages are among the most mysterious images in the whole of the mediæval English poetry. The planetary deities of Henryson, Douglas and Lydgate hardly compare. For figures as mysterious as Lygurge and Emetreus, uniting imagery of so many different kinds (astrological, physiognomic, psychological, emblematic, moral and sensuous) in so original and exploratory a manner, we have to turn to Elizabethan poetry, or to sixteenth-century engraved Temperament series—to Spenser, or to the Dürer of *Melencolia I*. The mysteriousness of Lygurge and Emetreus, however, is clearly enough of the kind that results from psychological depth. It may well be that they are not to be fully understood. But if we are to try to understand them, it must be as powers at work in Palamon and Arcite, and not as instances of nobility.

IV

That Palamon and Arcite ally themselves with Lygurge and Emetreus for the tournament can only mean that at this stage they have assimilated and can call upon the psychological qualities represented by the two kings. Arcite's choleric complexion under Martian-Solar influence is abundantly in evidence throughout the tale. His devotion to Mars, shown in his prayer at that god's temple and in his entry at the tournament under Scorpio, has already been noticed. We can now see, however, that Arcite is devoted, more precisely, to Mars in aspect with Sol. The temple murals show several activities characteristic of that particular influence (notably, "The cook yscalded, for al his longe ladel"), and when Arcite returns from his prayer he is "as fayn as fowel is of the brighte sonne" (l. 2437). Moreover, some of Emetreus's choleric attributes reappear associated with Arcite—notably, the horse. Arcite's steed as he went to do his May observance was "a courser, startlynge as the fir." Significantly, his choleric complexion was then extreme enough to distort his view of the real powers at work in his nature: at a time when he might be expected to have thoughts only for love, and when the narrator explicitly states—at some length, indeed— that the lover's heart has been overcast by "geery Venus" to make his mood as changeable as her day Friday (ll. 1530–39), it was not to Venus but to jealous Juno and "felle Mars" (l. 1559) that Arcite prayed. True, he acknowledged that Love had struck his heart through with his "firy dart so brennyngly" (l. 1564); but with no suggestion that he thought of love as a divine power. Just as on the occasion of his first falling in love he described the event as merely human, so now he apostrophized Emelye, not Venus; "Ye sleen me with youre eyen, Emelye! / Ye been the cause wherfor that I dye" (l. 1567f.).

Earlier, when he was sent into exile, Arcite suffered, the narrator tells us, from a lover's melancholy. It was not, however, the ordinary love-sickness called Hereos,

> but rather lyk manye,
> Engendred of humour malencolik,
> Biforen, in his celle fantastik.
>
> (ll. 1374–76)

The specific, even technical, character of the language of this passage encourages us to see an equally specific psychological implication. Mania was the term used in medicine for one particular form of melancholy, the choleric—"si ex colera [melancholia], tunc vocatur proprie mania." Thus Arcite's malady, which demonstrates like his death the unrecognized power of Saturn, is a malady possible only in one of extreme choleric complexion. As D. W. Robertson remarks, it was a dreaded affliction involving radical disorder of the patient's imagination and even, perhaps, of his moral judgment; so that it is hard to think that the pilgrims were invited to identify with Arcite, however much they might pity him.

Palamon, by contrast, shows no symptoms of excessive choler. From the outset he is devoted to Venus, whose power he rightly sees at work in his love for Emelye. (When he first falls in love with Emelye he even takes her for a form of the goddess.) In accordance with this Venerean influence, he enjoys a sanguinic complexion— the morally superior one, according to the commonest mediæval belief. In prison, Palamon suffers under the contrary influence, that of Saturn, god of prisons. Unlike Arcite, however, he can recognize the gods into whose power he has fallen:

> "I moot been in prisoun thurgh Saturne,
> And eek thurgh Juno, jalous and eek wood,
>
> . . . .
>
> And Venus sleeth me on that oother syde."
>
> (ll. 1328–32)

This passage occurs in a long complaint, which shows that Saturn's influence has taught Palamon to philosophize, at least to the point of adopting a *contemptus mundi* attitude. There is also something like a submission to Saturn in Palamon's calm acknowledgment that his destiny may be as a prisoner: "And if so be my destynee be shapen / By eterne word to dyen in prisoun" (l. 1108f.). In other words, whereas Arcite acknowledges only his own ruling deity, Palamon learns to temper his devotion to Venus with submission to reality's other powers. His cruel seven-year imprisonment in darkness—described by the narrator as a "martirdom"—eventually drives Palamon mad too. But in his case the temporary madness is a simple love-melancholy.

The resulting moral distinction between Palamon and Arcite is complete, and is manifested at almost every stage of the tale. It is not, however, a crude moral contrast: the Knight is too experienced and too well-bred for that. Consequently readers and even critics have been able to misunderstand his intention. We confine ourselves to three salient points of differentiation between the two lovers.

First, the confusion of Arcite's moral values is displayed in his betrayal of Palamon when he first falls in love. Palamon not only saw Emelye before Arcite did, but also confided his love (ll. 1093–1111). Arcite's duty as sworn friend and confidant, therefore, is to help Palamon. Instead, he claims freedom to love Emelye on his own account. In reply to reminders of his oath and accusations of treachery, he jeers at the exalted character of Palamon's love (ll. 1153–59); openly asserts a readiness to break "positif lawe" for the sake of the love he himself pursues (ll. 1162–71); and concludes with the amoral declaration, "Ech man for hymself, ther is noon oother" (l. 1182). Later this argument is repeated for emphasis, when Palamon, escaped from prison, overhears Arcite's soliloquy of love and addresses him as "false traytour wikke" (l. 1580). Again Arcite does not deny the charge, but fierce as the choleric lion (l. 1598) replies in amoral terms: "thynk wel that love is free" (l. 1606). The full wrong that he is doing to Palamon is not understood unless one recalls that in the Middle Ages promises were really supposed to be kept, and that in any case the value of love was inferior to that of friendship. But the tale reminds us of this ideal of friendship by introducing the legend of Pirithous and Theseus, an ancient exemplum of *felix concordia*. The relation of the true friends Perotheus and Theseus may at first appear to be in simple contrast with that of Arcite and Palamon. Theseus was prepared to descend into hell's prison for Perotheus's sake (l. 1200); unlike Arcite, who let Palamon languish in prison until another unnamed friend (l. 1468) helped him escape. But closer examination shows a more complex analogy. Pirithous and Theseus, like Arcite and Palamon, were friends whose love grew out of conflict. And the fact that it is Arcite whom Chaucer's Perotheus assists, rather than Palamon, may well allude to the legendary Pirithous's denial of a brother's claim.

Secondly, the prayers before the tournament show Palamon's moral superiority no less decisively. Arcite prays primarily for personal success in battle: "Yif me victorie, I aske thee namoore" (l. 2420). When he mentions love and Venus, it is significantly to her adultery that he refers, and to the dominating power of Mars's lustful victory over her. The licentiousness of the diction is unmistakable, and in context shocking:

> thow usedest the beautee
> Of faire, yonge, fresshe Venus free,
> And haddest hire in armes at thy wille.
>
> (ll. 2385–87)

Palamon, on the contrary, explicitly renounces victory—"Ne I ne axe nat tomorwe to have victorie" (l. 2239)—praying instead that he may "have fully possessioun / Of Emelye" (l. 2242f.). And though he refers to Venus's love for Adonis (l. 2224), he omits any allusion to her adultery, addressing her rather as "spouse of Vulcanus" (l. 2222). The contrast here is sharp. Arcite's prayer for victory shows his short-sightedness: he cannot see beyond the glory of battle to the deeper implications of union with Emelye. Palamon, however, can see that union as more than a victory, and knows that Venus's power is greater than Mars's (ll. 2248–50). He has learned, as Arcite obviously has not, that Mars must be bound by Venus. Moreover, in looking to the "end" of his desire rather than to any immediate event, he shows that he has learned from Saturn the virtue of perseverance. In addition, his more submissive and thoughtful prayer manifests a readiness for that perfection and completion of experience which is the province of the god of time.

Finally, there is a direct contrast between Palamon and Arcite in what was, to a mediæval audience, the critical matter of pride. The humility of Palamon's prayer has already been remarked. He has no interest in "renoun in this cas, ne veyne glorie / Of pris of armes blowen up and doun" (l. 2240f.). Arcite's contrary prayer for glory—a rather insolent one in tone—is in keeping with his behaviour outside the temple of Mars. Thus, to Palamon's first accusation of betrayal, Arcite replies "ful proudly" (l. 1152). And he loses his life after the tournament while parading his victory, enacting what would have been recognized by the Knight's audience as an emblem of *Superbia*. Lacking the discipline and prudence of Palamon, Arcite, who inclines too much to the impetuous rigour of the choleric, has fallen into vainglory.

In short, it is as far as possible from the truth to say, as Robertson does, that Palamon's condition differs from Arcite's "only in degree." The difference is qualitative, both morally and psychologically, and it is so extreme that Palamon's eventual winning of Emelye should be felt as poetic justice.

Nevertheless, Arcite's supersession is not felt quite in this way. For it is also true that from the beginning the two lovers have been very closely twinned. We can even sympathize, to some extent, with the casual reader who finds it hard to distinguish them. Thus, Palamon and Arcite are closely related members of one family; at the sack of Thebes they are found, both insensible, in the same heap of wounded "Bothe in oon armes, wroght ful richely" (l. 1012); at the tournament they appear at the "selve moment" (l. 2584); and the exact evenness of their forces "withouten variacioun" is the theme of a long and emphatic passage (ll. 2587–94). Besides, the moral contrast between Palamon and Arcite is by no means schematic or unrelieved. A defence of Arcite's character, though it would be misguided, would not be a ridiculous or hopelessly perverse undertaking. On occasion he is by no means lacking in magnanimity and honour—as witness his succour of the weakened Palamon at lines 1608–19, or the true nobility of his dying words. After Arcite's death, moreover, Palamon thinks him worth mourning. Indeed, his grief is prolonged and almost inconsolable.

All these apparently conflicting features of the tale can be reconciled, however, if it is seen as a symbolic representation of character development. Palamon's grief is so extreme because he has, as it were, witnessed the passing of a part of himself—the Martian, choleric part—his early youth. He may recognize the discipline maturity demanded: he may ally himself with the lawgiver Lygurge: but that does not diminish a chivalric knight's regret for the passing of youth's freedom and glory. Arcite's moving speech at the point of death confirms this interpretation, for he comes at the end to see the vanity of his desires ("what asketh men to have"), to confess his own choleric "strif and rancour . . . and . . . jalousye" and to recognize Palamon as "the gentil man" (ll. 2777, 2784ff., 2797). At that point, when he acknowledges the superiority of Palamon's values, he is reunited with him and at the same time ceases to exist. His separate existence, indeed, is now superfluous: the conflict over, his better qualities are incorporated in the lover who survives, the more mature stage of the supercharacter Palamon-Arcite-Emetreus-Lygurge. In Daniel Richter's words,

> If you want to be a man
> You must kill a boy.

It may be asked why, in that case, the gods should permit Arcite to be the winner of the tournament, however briefly. Why should Palamon ever have been bound by Arcite and his supporters, when it was Venus who ought to have bound Mars? The answer can again be given in terms of character formation and the sequence of ages. In schemes of the Ages of Man—both in four-age and in seven-age schemes—the choleric Martian and Solar phase intervened between the earlier Venerean (sanguinic) and the later Saturnian (melancholic). Thus we may think of the tale's super-character as passing out of sanguinic youth, through an all-too-brief sunny prime or "flour" of martial success, into the Third or Middle Age. In terms of generated characters, the Venerean Palamon—Palamon as supported in heaven by Venus—is inevitably defeated by the representative of the next phase, the Martian Arcite. But time (Saturn) has a further surprise in store. The Martian Arcite is himself in turn overthrown through Saturn's agency, i.e., by a further lapse of time ("by processe and by lengthe of certeyn yeres")—being superseded by a changed Palamon who has become very much the child of Saturn. Significantly, the tale's last description of Palamon is of a *Tristitia* or *Melancholia* figure:

> Tho cam this woeful Theban Palamoun,
> With flotery berd and ruggy, asshy heeres,
> In clothes blake, ydropped al with teeres.
>
> (ll. 2882–84)

Only in the last resort, with Saturn's help, is Venus stronger than Mars. Only with the long passage of time (repeatedly dwelt on throughout the tale) can love grow out of passion and wilful free-dom, or come to the maturity of lawful stable marital relation.

V

Fitting Emelye and Theseus into the above theory of the Knight's Tale is a matter of greater delicacy. Both characters show subtly conflicting tendencies in respect of their maturity. This does not seem to reflect any indecision, however, on the part of the poet, but is rather designed to betray an ambivalence in the narrator.

Emelye most obviously represents the phlegmatic complexion (the complexion in a sense of all women, regardless of age), associated usually with Luna though sometimes also with Venus. Palamon's final attainment of union with Emelye is in accordance with this identification, since the phlegmatic was commonly the complexion of the last age of man. That age of man was of course rheumy and unpleasant—a time "whan his name apalled is for age, / For al forgoten is his vasselage" (l. 3053f.). Yet none the less its equanimity might also be seen as a not unworthy goal of moral effort. As we have said, Emelye's uniting elements of Diana and of Venus constituted an ideal of moderation. And her family relation with the Jovian Theseus further supports such an interpretation, since Jupiter and Luna were the two mediating planets in the astrology of the time.

On the other hand, what we have seen of Emelye's movement to maturity suggests a somewhat different interpretation. Her marriage to Palamon is from her own point of view a union with the knight of Venus. It completes a transference from Diana's patronage to Venus's that began in her prayer before the tournament, and allowed the generative goddess to fulfil her purpose through the temporal means of Saturn. This interpretation also has a basis in scheme. For Venus was more often associated with the sanguinic complexion than with the phlegmatic, and a common arrangement of the Ages ran:

Phlegmatic	Sanguinic	Choleric	Melancholic	Phlegmatic
Childhood	Youth	Prime	Middle Age	Second Childhood
Luna	Venus, Jupiter	Mars	Saturn	Luna

Moreover, in the seven-age scheme Venus again governed a later age than that of Luna:

LUNA	MERCURIUS	VENUS	SOL	MARS	JUPITER	SATURNUS
Infantia	Pueritia	Adolescentia	Iuventus	Virilis	Senilis	Senecta et decrepita

It will be noted that this interpretation of Emelye places a high evaluation on the sanguinic complexion, that associated also with Jupiter. In the Middle Ages, as we have already remarked, the sanguinic complexion was often regarded as morally preferable.

It is Theseus's character, however, that is presented most ambivalently. To a superficial view—and for the most part the narrator's own view is in agreement—Theseus grows to maturity like the other characters. After Arcite's death, for example, Theseus has the benefit of Egeus's advice about Time the healer. He learns that the resolution that he (and Jupiter) cannot accomplish by busyness, Saturn can bring about by the lapse of slow time. Theseus's consequent passage from the Jovian Sixth Age to the Saturnian Seventh appears to form the climax of the tale, in his long speech acknowledging time's function in the ultimate workings of the universe:

> He [the Prime Mover] hath so wel biset his ordinaunce,
> That speces of thynges and progressiouns
> Shullen enduren by successiouns,
> And nat eterne, withouten any lye.
>
> (ll. 3012–15)

But a deeper scrutiny suggests that Theseus remains oddly impervious to Egeus's advice, so that it can actually be said, inappropriately enough, to "gladen" him (l. 2837). His response to sentiments about the transitoriness of life's pilgrimage is not *contemptus mundi* but only more busyness, more plans, more practical activity: "Duc Theseus, with al his bisy cure / Caste now wher that the sepulture / . . . may best ymaked be" (ll. 2853–55). Yet again officers run to execute his commands. And even his speech before the Athenian parliament, though spoken with sad visage from a breast called wise (l. 2183), represents imperfect submission to Saturn. It is Theseus's deepest, most considered judgment, delivered with Saturnian slowness and weight. It formally acknowledges the power of mutability. Yet it nevertheless betrays an incomplete detachment, by mediæval standards, from the world and from Jupiter, to whose necessity it ascribes the real power. The "First Moevere" may decree that the oak (Jupiter's tree!) shall endure only by succession and be "nat eterne," but somehow this is still Jupiter's doing:

> "What maketh this but Juppiter, the kyng,
> That is prince and cause of alle thyng."
>
> (l. 3035f.)

Incorrigibly Jovial, Theseus to the end makes "vertu of necessitee" (l. 3042): his secular stoicism is saddened and deepened, not abandoned.

This is surprising, even disturbing, in face of Theseus's special role as the tale's ideal character. The story is told from a point of view that Theseus alone, of all its characters, would find it possible to share. Adopting a transformational approach analogous to that of Chomsky's, we might imagine the same story related from Egeus's point of view, say, or Palamon's. In the latter—told perhaps by the Squire—love would be treated with absolute solemnity. But in the story we have, told by the Knight, even Palamon's love is subjected (l. 1798ff.) to the same benign, tolerant, jovial irony that pervades almost all the narrative, and that, if style had been our subject, would have been a main concern of the present paper. Only Theseus has the narrator's full and evident sympathy.

Yet Theseus, though a formidable character of many strengths, is never completely satisfactory from a moral standpoint. It is not only during the final stage of the story that he falls short of the ideal: throughout he manifests an individuality faulty both in attitude and in behaviour. We notice especially a hard, angry, pitiless rigour more Martian than Jovial. When he discovers Palamon and Arcite fighting Theseus "quook and sterte" with ire (l. 1762), and the whole company of ladies has to get down on their "bare knees" on the ground before he will relent (l. 1758). Understandably enough, his long service of Mars has left him hard, though not, in the end, unyielding. It seems that we are to think of him as being in process of transition from the age of Mars to that of Jupiter: his choleric tendencies are still only with difficulty subdued. As late as the tournament, he shows himself more Martian than Saturnian. Thus, in planning the temples at the lists he conspicuously omits a temple to Saturn. (This would have been very noticeable at a time when the Four Ages and their associated complexions and deities were often portrayed as quadrants of a circle.) And earlier, we recall, there were oaths by Mars and a Martian banner.

All this is intelligible if, and only if, the character of the narrator himself is taken into account. Theseus seems an ideal figure to the Knight because the Knight shares his faults and to some extent his virtues. It is natural, for example, that a knight who has been "at many a noble armee" and fought in fifteen battles (Gen. Prol. l. 60f.) should look to victory and to Mars. The Knight's service of Mars is often in evidence in the tale—most obviously, perhaps, when he has the dying Arcite, pray almost with his last words "Juppiter so wys my soule gye" (l. 2786), then within a few lines comments, in his own person, "Arcite is coold, ther Mars his soule gye!" (l. 2815). Understandable, too, in a soldier, even a crusader, is a certain jovial secularity and stoicism of attitude. Luck is inevitably important to him: as Petrarch put it, Fortune is "in battaglia potentissima." So it is appropriately by lot that the Knight begins the storytelling. And it is a highly appropriate stance that he should exclaim: "welcome be the cut, a Goddes name!" (Gen. Prol. l. 854). For the Knight's God, like Theseus's, is Jupiter *Fortuna maiora*. The other gods he portrays, on the whole, as tricky, dangerous and malevolent, if not quite as evil as D. W. Robertson has it. Sometimes his view is strikingly partial, as when he makes Saturn say "I slow Sampsoun, shakynge the piler" (1. 2466), as if the death of Samson had never been regarded as anything but a sinister catastrophe. To the Knight, the other gods are for the most part enemies of Jupiter's secular order, which has to be maintained, or even fought for, against them.

The Knight's Tale would gain much poignancy if it were regarded, in some such way as we have proposed, as an expression appropriate to a particular stage of its narrator's life. The Knight may be conscious that his own career as a soldier is far advanced, even near its end. With whatever reluctance, he must face the onset of age and the necessity of turning to a more peaceful occupation. It is perhaps no accident that he tells a story in which outgrowing the choleric Martian age bulks so largely—in which war passes in the process of time to formal combat à l'outrance, then to tournament, and finally to peace. For we have to think of the wise "meeke" (Gen. Prol. 1. 69) Knight as being himself in passage from the Sixth to the Seventh Age. Perhaps going on the pilgrimage has for him a more serious meaning than for some of the other pilgrims.

As we would interpret the Knight's Tale, its meaning is neither general expression of chivalric nobility nor portrayal of the evil of passionate involvements. It is meant to convey something of the order underlying the unpredictable changes of human destiny: of growth to wise maturity through a succession of ages and attitudes; of the soul's formation and ascent through a series of planetary stages. Within its four parts it attempts to box the whole compass of human life, aiming at a comprehensive irony that will embrace all attitudes more extreme and less mature. Yet it is also, like the other *Canterbury Tales,* told from an individual, dramatic point of view. Its schemes have the effect, not of definitive universal conventions, but of tentative exploratory essays. They seem to form the scaffolding of self-understanding at a particular stage of development, and as such to make possible new access and fresh ordering of experience. The result is a position worthy of deep respect, but also, inevitably, one partial and relative in its truth. It is noble and comprehensive enough to be surpassed in scope only by the sermon that concludes the *Canterbury Tales.* Then at last, in the Parson's call to repentance for all mortal life, with its scheme of seven sins and answering virtues, the Knight's secular vision of seven ages and planetary guardians finds its superior divine counterpart.

Tale of Civil Conduct

Donald R. Howard

The Knight's Tale introduces three thematic strains related to three realms of human conduct: the civil, the domestic, and the private. These were the three areas in which worldly authority was called for—the state or nation, the family or home, and the individual will. The appropriate authority figures are the king or ruler, the husband or father, and the church or conscience.

The major theme of the Knight's Tale is the major theme of all medieval romance—chivalry. Whatever else it may be, the Knight's Tale is a projection about the noble life. It praises valor in warfare, courtesy and honor in interpersonal relationships, and the fame or "glory" which was thought the just reward of noble deeds. The two prisoners in the tale love the same lady; when one escapes and the other is exiled, they come upon each other accidentally in a forest and engage in furious battle. Arcite, in the chivalric spirit, will not fight Palamon until he gets food for him and armor. The battle is stopped by the duke Theseus, who imposes civil restrictions: it must be made a game, a tournament with rules, blunted weapons, and ritual. And the winner of the tournament, Arcite, when the gods take his prize away from him, resigns the lady to the rival in a self-sacrificing manner appropriate to (it is his own word) a "gentleman."

A part of this ethos is the idealized love for the distant and

From *The Idea of the* Canterbury Tales. © 1976 by the Regents of the University of California. University of California Press, 1976.

indifferent lady which sets the two young prisoners at odds; this love is in no way conceived as an adulterous relationship—its end, in the minds of the lovers and in fact, is marriage. Later we are to have a group of tales on marriage and domestic life.

The Knight's Tale introduces not only these civil and domestic realms of conduct, but the private realm of thought and moral choice. It is a philosophical romance into which its teller injects chivalric and religious conceptions. The principle of Fortune's Wheel, the principle of the Chain of Love, and the notion that we can make virtue of necessity by resignation are familiar medieval ideas drawn from Boethius. This "Boethian" element in the Knight's Tale has been endlessly remarked on and is its most evident intellectual feature. But the Knight intellectualizes in other respects too: at the end of his first section, for example, he raises a courtly *demande d'amour* of the kind medieval aristocrats evidently liked to entertain: "You lovers axe I now this questioun: / Who hath the worse, Arcite or Palamon?" (ll. 1347–48; line numbers conform to F. N. Robinson, 2d ed.). And he includes details about the ancient world, the pagan gods, astrology, medicine, and so on. We can view these as his private thoughts and opinions, his mental content. But it should not surprise us that his mental content has much in common with what we might expect from any knight.

The Knight's learning comes not, as a clerk's learning would have, from books, but from a body of lore some of which was preserved in books but most of which was probably passed on orally. It is useful when we think of medieval oral traditions to suppose that there were separate traditions for separate groups—a "folklore" of the people, a "knightlore" of the aristocracy, a "clerklore" among churchmen. Since churchmen were the literate segment of the society, we can suppose that more clerklore was written down than knightlore and folklore. This fact has helped create the impression that all medieval art and thought is religious, but the impression is not true and the Knight's tale shows it is not: the things the Knight thinks about are in part religious, but not exclusively so. He is interested in questions of honor, courtesy, and valor; in lists, weapons, armor, tactics—in what Othello called the "quality, pride, pomp, and circumstance of glorious war." He is interested in the pageantry of warfare, in the fame or glory due the individual warrior, "service" to a lady, and noble last words. He tells a story set in a pagan world, and admires in his pagan characters those qualities which make them chivalric and philosophical. The forces of destiny in his tale impose order on what would otherwise seem haphazard events; this is also an intellectual construct, even a scientific one, for it involves the stars. When Arcite has won the battle, a "fury infernal" (1. 2684) makes his horse leap aside and founder; this would seem a trivial, even ridiculous incident if the fury were not sent at the behest of Saturn. That such destinal order exists in the universe is often taken as the theme of the tale. The lore which the Knight possesses involves an epic and fatalistic way of looking at things, which is probably the way soldiers need to see life if they are to go on being soldiers.

Chaucer also introduced into the Knight's Tale the limitation to the secular world which he imposed on the work as a whole. In the *Troilus* we saw the hero translated into a timeless realm from which he looks upon the world, but in the *Canterbury Tales* we never pass out of the world or out of time. This limitation is introduced at the key scene of the Knight's Tale, the death of Arcite. In a famous anticlimax the author makes a point of omitting the soul journey through the spheres which was in his source:

> Dusked his eyen two, and failed breeth.
> But on his lady yet cast he his eye;
> His laste word was, "Mercy, Emelye!"
> His spirit chaunged house and wente ther
> As I came never, I can nat tellen wher.
> Therefore I stinte, I nam no divinistre.
>
> (ll. 2806-11)

Once Arcite is dead we must cast our eyes away from him and examine the survivors, for we are on the pilgrimage of human life and the span of our vision is limited to it.

In such speeches as this one Chaucer also introduced a jocular and exaggerated element that seems to call the Knight's convictions into question. For example, while the two heroes are fighting he says "in this wise I let hem fighting dwelle" and turns his attention to Theseus:

> The destinee, ministre general,
> That executeth in the world over all
> The purveiaunce that God hath seen biforn,
> So strong it is that, though the world had sworn

> The contrary of a thing by ye or nay,
> Yet sometime it shall fallen on a day
> That falleth nat eft within a thousand yeer.
> For certainly, our appetites here,
> Be it of wer, or pees, or hate, or love,
> All is this ruled by the sight above.
> This mene I now by mighty Theseus,
> That for to hunten is so desirous,
> And namely at the grete hert in May,
> That in his bed there daweth him no day
> That he nis clad, and redy for to ride
> With hunt and horn and houndes him biside.
> For in his hunting hath he swich delit
> That it is all his joy and appetit
> To been himself the grete hertes bane.
> For after Mars he serveth now Diane.
>
> (ll. 1663–82)

All this machinery is intended to let us know that on a certain day Theseus took it in mind to go hunting. It is impossible not to see a mock-epic quality in such a passage, and hard not to conclude that its purpose is ironic, that it is meant to put us at a distance from the Knight's grandiose ideas of destiny and make us think about them. This humorous element in the Knight's Tale is the most controversial aspect of the tale: where one critic writes it off as an "antidote" to tragedy another puts it at the center of things, but no one denies it is there. It introduces a feature which we will experience in many a tale: we read the tale as a dramatic monologue spoken by its teller but understand that some of Chaucer's attitudes spill into it. This feature gives the tale an artistry which we cannot realistically attribute to the teller: I am going to call this *unimpersonated artistry*. In its simplest form it is the contingency that a tale not memorized but told impromptu is in verse. The artistry is the author's, though selected features of the pilgrim's dialect, argot, or manner may still be impersonated. In its more subtle uses it allows a gross or "low" character to use language, rhetoric, or wit above his capabilities. (Sometimes it is coupled with an impersonated *lack* of art, an artlessness or gaucherie which causes a character to tell a bad tale, as in Sir Thopas, or to violate literary conventions or proprieties, as in the Knight's Tale.) The effect is that of irony or parody, but this effect is Chaucer's accomplishment, not an impersonated skill for which the pilgrim who tells the tale deserves any compliments.

The "I" in the Knight's Tale who provides this unimpersonated artistry has always been a riddle. One kind of "I" occurs in the descriptions of the temples, where the Knight begins to speak as if he himself had been an eyewitness—

> There saugh I first the derk imagining
> Of Felony, and all the compassing.
>
> (ll. 1995–96)

> Yet saugh I Woodness, laughinge in his rage.
>
> (l. 2011)

> Saugh I Conquest, sitting in greet honour.
>
> (l. 2028)

> Now to the temple of Diane the chaste,
> As shortly as I can, I wol me haste.
>
> (ll. 2051–52)

Chaucer had this from Boccaccio; it is a familiar rhetorical device of the Middle Ages—the nonpersonal "I" which Leo Spitzer described, a kind of Everyman. But when Chaucer uses another rhetorical device (*occupatio*) to condense his original, we get an "I" who is not the Knight and not a faceless Everyman, but an author. The most famous example, if one can judge fame by measuring footnotes, is line 1201: "But of that story list me nat to write."

This "I" who writes is certainly Chaucer, not the Knight; the only question is, whether the line was included by mistake or for an artistic purpose. It is often argued that such passages are leftovers from an earlier version not intended for the *Canterbury Tales*. Thus Professor Williams reminds us that "We of the twentieth century . . . may not quite appreciate the difficulties of revision in an age when writers used various scraps of paper, vellum, parchment, and even wax tablets for their work, and scribbled with muddy ink, a feather quill, and no professionally fitted spectacles, in the dim candlelight of drafty closets." Are we then to believe that Chaucer, who was not a stranger to revision, took from his files the first of the Canterbury tales and inserted it without even reading it? If his notion was that every line in every tale should sound like its teller in style and manner, if each tale was to be a dramatic monologue pure and simple, wouldn't he have struck out such passages of ironic self-humor? Any quill pen dipped in some muddy ink would have done it without any difficulty. Or are we to believe that in the dim candlelight and without proper spectacles he didn't notice such a line? Suppose instead that at some level of consciousness Chaucer in this instance intended his *own* voice (not the naive narrator's) to intrude into the Knight's Tale. The effect is not so peculiar if he wrote for oral delivery and included the model of performance in the work: to listeners the author's presence was never forgotten—everyone knew the pilgrims were all roles being played by the poet. Even fourteenth-century *readers* (the Man of Law is an example put before us in the work itself) would have known the author's identity and felt his presence, as we still do.

But if we say this happens, what are we to say it accomplishes? The "I" who writes is bored with writing: after describing Arcite's suffering, for example, he asks "What shold I all day of his woe endite?" (l. 1380). Sometimes he appears to be making fun of the narrative, as when he describes Palamon's imprisonment (ll. 1454–68). He permits moving and dramatic speeches to end abruptly with a curious anticlimactic ring—for example, Arcite's beautiful lament (ll. 1563–71), a moving and courtly utterance, is followed with this bit of stage business:

> And with that word he fell down in a trance
> A longe time, and after he up sterte.

At one point Chaucer shows the heroes fighting ankle-deep in their own blood—a circumstance hard to arrange even in a bathtub—and adds "And in this wise I let hem fighting dwelle" (l. 1661). The most famous examples come at the very climax of the story, the death of Arcite:

> All is tobrosten thilke regioun;
> Nature hath no dominacioun.
> And certainly, ther Nature wol nat werche,
> Farewell physik! go beer the man to chirche!
>
> (ll. 2757–60)

Obviously the purpose is satiric or parodic. As the Knight tells his perfectly serious tale, an "I" emerges; this "I" selects, condenses, writes. He finds the tale not quite so high-minded—finds it unwieldy, sometimes silly—and he permits some of its most dramatic moments to collapse into moments of irony, even into farce or "camp." Who else can this be but the author? The problem is to decide, if we can, what he may be satirizing and how serious a criticism this satire is meant to be. And the trouble is that we cannot be sure until we have read on—until we have got through the Melibee, the Nun's Priest's Tale, the Manciple's Tale—and attained a better sense of the author's frame of mind in its broadest dimensions. To get ahead of myself, I will say that I think Chaucer is satirizing not the Knight himself but the knightly mentality, including its literary tastes, and that he is satirizing it with delicate irony—is satirizing something for which he had respect.

The Knight represents the dominant class in medieval society, and his tale is a composite picture of its mentality. The very form of the tale, with its elaborate symmetry and stately, ritual progression, reflects the medieval knights' love of pageantry and game. And the great emphasis in the tale is upon valor or prowess—the knight's ability to vanquish a foe in battle. This value of the medieval knighthood is symbolically represented in Arcite, the "Martian" character: it is set in opposition to the other knightly value, love. Because Palamon symbolizes this phase of medieval knightly preoccupations (he is Venus's knight) the rivalry of the two heroes represents that bit of knightlore which made the lady's love a reward of knightly valor. The lady herself is a distant and unreal figure: she never speaks except in prayer—to the goddess of chastity. It is probably typical of chivalric idealism that this reward, coming at the climactic moment of the story after Arcite has won the battle, is offered in the exiguous form which knights in romances desired: a friendly look.

> And she again him cast a freendlich eye
> (For women, as to speken in commune,
> They follwen all the favour of Fortune)
> And she was all his cheer, as in his herte.
>
> (ll. 2680–83)

It is probably typical of the chivalric spirit, too, that the changeableness of women is underscored here, for the world of chivalry was a man's world and a lady's favor was a man's reward, something he won and possessed—she was, we learn, *his* delight in *his* heart. (I prefer this reading of line 2683, which Donaldson gives, to

"And was al his, in chiere, as in his herte" [Baugh] or "And was al his chiere, as in his herte" [Manly-Rickert, Robinson]. If "chiere" means countenance, not cheer or delight as I take it, the reading "in chiere" must be adopted, but the thrust of the passage is undisturbed—the sense would be that she was his in her appearance or look, as [much as] in his heart.) The other reward of knightly valor was fame. The "Boethian" speeches at the end are often allowed to overshadow the fact that after Boethius has had his say Theseus confers fame upon Arcite, offering a rationale for dying at the height of one's powers:

> And certainly a man hath most honour
> To dien in his excellence and flowr,
> Whan he is siker of his goode name;
> Than hath he doon his freend, ne him, no shame.
> And gladder ought his freend been of his deeth,
> Whan with honour up yolden is his breeth,
> Than whan his name apaled is for age,
> For all forgetten is his vassellage.
> Than is it best, as for a worthy fame,
> To dien whan that he is best of name.

(ll. 3047–56)

A favorable marriage is part of this chivalric system: at the end Palamon is "living in bliss, in richesse, and in heele" (l. 3102). The marriage is a happy marriage without jealousy "or any other tene" (l. 3106). As a cultural ideal this was a very secular one: knights strove for victory to attain rewards far from spiritual—"richesse" is among them.

The operation of the planets, which provides the celestial machinery creaking behind the plot and coming up with a convenient emergency, is a mirror image of the plot itself: the planets are gods, and therefore a super-race of nobles—a ruling class which rules the ruling class. The strife between Palamon and Arcite (lover and warrior) is reflected in the heavens by the strife between Venus and Mars. Against these dazzling figures, the goddess Diana is as shadowy as her devotee Emelye. A powerful male figure, Saturn, grandfather of Venus, intervenes and settles things as Theseus does below. The two kings who fight for Palamon and Arcite, Lygurge and Emetreus, have been shown to represent the Saturnalian and Martian characters respectively: in them we see the outcome shaping up as we see the armies gather. But the celestial plot is scarcely idealized—the gods bicker and dicker like humans, each has a vested interest, they form alliances, and the outcome depends on power (and seniority) rather than on right.

While this over-plot goes on in the sky, the armies gather below:

> For every wight that loved chivalrye,
> And wold, his thankes, han a passant name,
> Hath prayed that he might been of that game;
> And well was him that thereto chosen was.
> For if there fill tomorrwe swich a cas,
> Ye knowen well that every lusty knight
> That loveth paramours and hath his might,
> Were it in Engelond or elleswhere,
> They wold, hir thankes, wilnen to be there—
> To fighten for a lady, *benedicitee*!
> It were a lusty sighte for to see.
>
> (ll. 2106–16)

This picture of knights coming from all over the world to fight for someone else's lady suggests very strongly that their first love was the fighting. The battle is central, yet the attitudes of the three principles, revealed in their prayers, differ. They belong to a warrior class for whom war is the central action in life, but each *thinks* differently. Palamon does not care whether he has victory or not "so that I have my lady in myn armes" (l. 2247). Arcite can see no further than victory, and the statue of Mars promises him that in a single word (l. 2433). The heroine, like a good medieval lady, wishes first chastity, and, failing that, whoever desires her most. The story presents fundamental passions of love and aggression which reduce the principals to an animal-like state; the imagery used of them, drawn from Boethius, enforces this conception and reveals a degeneration in them. But the knights are saved from this descent into animal behavior by the ruler's imposition of a code. Theseus demands proper civil conduct: the thing must be done fair and square, and the gods (or planets) join in to bring this about.

It is hard to say whether Chaucer viewed the Knight's tale, despite its mannerisms, sympathetically. The Knight himself was presented in the General Prologue as a noble, indeed ideal figure, though from an older order that no longer examined its assumptions. In the tale, civil virtues give the characters and their actions dignity. But this civility is, as perhaps with all imposed codes, an artifice.

"The Struggle between Noble Designs and Chaos": The Literary Tradition of Chaucer's Knight's Tale

Robert W. Hanning

There is perhaps no better illustration of the processes of continuity and change in medieval literature than the relationship between Geoffrey Chaucer's Knight's Tale (1386?), first of the *Canterbury Tales,* and its literary antecedents, both proximate—Giovanni Boccaccio's *Teseida delle nozze d'Emilia* (ca. 1340)—and remote— the *Thebaid* of Statius (ca. 92 A.D.). Moreover, a comparison of Chaucer's poem with Statius's epic and Boccaccio's epic romance offers important clues to the meaning of one of the most problematic tales in the Canterbury collection.

To Boccaccio and Chaucer, and to medieval authors generally, Statius was *the* authority on the fall of Thebes, one of the most traumatic events of classical legend. Charles Muscatine, in the most influential, and perhaps the finest recent assessment of the Knight's Tale, states, "the history of Thebes had perpetual interest for Chaucer as an example of the struggle between noble designs and chaos," a struggle which Muscatine finds at the heart of the tale (*Chaucer and the French Tradition*). According to Muscatine, "the noble life . . . is itself the subject of the poem and the object of its philosophic questions," and the manifestations of that life, "its dignity and richness, its regard for law and decorum, are all bulwarks against the ever-threatening forces of chaos, and in constant collision with them." In this reading, the significance of the Knight's Tale lies in

From *The Literary Review* 23, no. 4 (Summer 1980). © 1980 by Fairleigh Dickinson University.

Theseus's "perception of the order beyond chaos," revealed in his final speech urging a distraught Palamon and Emelye to marry, despite their grief at the death of Arcite, and thus to conform to the scheme of the universe's "Firste Moevere." As Muscatine puts it, "when the earthly designs suddenly crumble, true nobility is faith in the ultimate order of all things."

The present essay responds to Muscatine's analysis of the Knight's Tale in two ways. First, it examines two main sources of Chaucer's attitude toward Thebes, in order to confirm the contention that the English poet found in Boccaccio and Statius models for "the struggle between noble designs and chaos"—found, that is, a tradition of concern with the tense relationship between the human capacity to control and order life and the forces, internal and external, that resist or negate order. But if Chaucer is profoundly traditional in composing the Knight's Tale, he is also profoundly original in telling it not *in propria voce,* but as the utterance of "a worthy man" and "a verray parfit gentil knyght"—an exponent of the "noble life" of chivalry as Chaucer and his age knew it. By putting the Knight between us and the world of Theseus, Palamon, Arcite, and Emelye, Chaucer invites us to see the conflict of order and disorder as a reflection of the Knight's particular perspective on life. The Knight's Tale thus becomes simultaneously a comment on the possibilities for order in human life and a comment on the tensions Chaucer perceived within the system of late medieval chivalry. Further, since the Knight makes us painfully aware of his difficulties as an amateur storyteller, Chaucer innovates again in inviting us to equate Theseus's problems in seeking to control the realm of experience with his pilgrim-creator's trials in seeking to control the realm of art. The coincidence of problems faced by Duke, gentil knight, and poet makes the Knight's Tale an even more complex and original poem than its most perceptive critics have noticed. Accordingly, an assessment of the tension between the tale's levels of meaning will constitute my second, more revisionist response to Muscatine's thesis.

I

The *Thebaid* recounts the fratricidal war between Oedipus's sons, Polynices and Eteocles, for the throne of Thebes. Its twelfth and last book contains the germ of Boccaccio's *Teseida,* and thus of the Knight's Tale. In the twelfth book, after the brothers have destroyed each other in a final, emblematic single combat, Creon, their uncle and now ruler of Thebes, forbids burial rites for Polynices and the Greek warriors who beseiged the city with him. The grief-stricken widows of the unburied, outraged at the sacrilegious edict but powerless to contest it, are advised by a Theban soldier to turn to Theseus, ruler of Athens, for succor. The greater part of book twelve comprises a double action attendant upon Creon's prohibition and the widows' response. Spurred on by desperation, Argia, the Greek widow of Polynices, and Antigone, Polynices' sister, attempt to perform funeral rites for the slain prince, defying the edict. They find the body and put it on a pyre with another, half-consumed corpse who turns out to be none other than Eteocles. Implacable foes in death as in life, the brothers resist the joint immolation; the fire divides into warring tongues of flame while the women watch in helpless terror. The posthumous struggle shakes the pyre, and the noise arouses Creon's guards, who apprehend Argia and Antigone and bring them before Creon to be executed—victims, it would seem, of yet another grotesque manifestation of the curse on the house of Cadmus. Meanwhile, the rest of the widows journey to Athens, where, under Juno's tutelage, they win the sympathy of the Athenians and encounter Theseus as he returns in triumph from Scythia, victor over the Amazons and lord of Hippolyta. He learns the cause of the widows' sorrow and, his army swollen by recruits enraged at Creon's behavior, sets out for Thebes. Creon learns of Theseus's arrival as he prepares to punish Argia and Antigone; despite his speech of defiance, his troops are no match for Theseus, who seeks out and dispatches the Theban tyrant. The epic ends on a muted note of grief and resignation as the widows perform the obsequies for their men.

The *Thebaid* offers a dark view of life, shaped as it is by a legend that stresses the inescapable destiny which destroys a family and leads to fratricidal wrath between its protagonists. Yet the last act of the epic incorporates a movement back from the abyss of rage and destruction, and toward a reestablishment of civilized control over the darker impulses that have reigned throughout. Theseus, whose intervention saves Argia and Antigone and allows the fallen warriors to have the funeral rites owed them by heroic society, represents the belated, partial, but real triumph of civilization over passion, both at Thebes and in Scythia. The image of

Hippolyta, brought back to Athens in triumph by Theseus, sums up his achievement and his function in the epic's economy: "Hippolyta too drew all toward her, friendly now in look and patient of the marriage-bond. With hushed whispers and sidelong gaze the Attic dames marvel that she has broken her country's austere laws, that her locks are trim, and all her bosom hidden beneath her robe, that though a barbarian she mingles with mighty Athens, and comes to bear offspring to her foeman-lord" (bk. 12, ll. 533–39, trans. J. H. Mozley). Every detail of this striking portrait testifies to the subduing of wildness by its opposite. The Amazon queen, sworn to enmity toward men, accustomed to flaunting her freedom from male (and social) restraint by her flowing hair, her dress with its one exposed breast (an affront to canons of feminine modesty), and her fierce demeanor, has become a neat, proper, smiling wife and mother-to-be. And as Theseus has tamed the savage Amazon, so will he tame the sacrilegious Creon, rescue Argia and Antigone from being punished for wishing to perform the rituals by which civilization imposes order even on death, and permit the comfort of those rituals to all the bereaved.

Of course, Theseus paradoxically quells rage and violence by unleashing his own, righteous wrath. In his speech to his soldiers as they set out for Thebes, he declares that they fight in a just cause, and against the Furies, emblems of primal chaos; then he hurls his spear and dashes forth on the road to the rage-torn city (bk. 12, ll. 642–49). This is no statesmanship of sweetness and light, but the sanctioned unleashing of irresistible energy to assure the triumph of "terrarum leges et mundi foedera"—the laws of nations and the covenants of the world (bk. 12, l. 642). A similar ambivalence hovers over Theseus's shield, on which is portrayed the hero binding the Minotaur on Crete, yet another emblem of terrifying force subjugated by a greater and more licit violence (bk. 12, ll. 665–76). All of these deeds of conquest take place away from home—in Scythia, at Thebes, on Crete; Athens, like the Rome of Virgil and Statius, remains the peaceful center of civilization, where mourning women are instructed by Juno in the proper decorum of grief (bk. 12, ll. 464–70), and where there is a temple dedicated to Clementia, the spirit of mildness and forgiveness.

Despite Theseus's authority and easy victory over Creon, there is still no erasing the terrible memory of the death and destruction which fate and the gods have rained down on Thebes throughout the epic, nor can any image of rage subdued by civilization—not even the domesticated Hippolyta—match for sheer evocative power the horror of that moment when the charred remains of Polynices and Eteocles continue in death the fratricidal fury that ruined their lives. Statius's vision of the noble life offers as its highest realization the double-tongued flame and trembling pyre, and the hysterical pleas of Argia and Antigone that the rage cease before it compels them to leap into the flames to separate the brothers (bk. 12, ll. 429–46). It was to such a pessimistic vision that Boccaccio, and later Chaucer, responded in taking up the poetic challenge of the *Thebaid*.

II

Writing over twelve hundred years after Statius, Giovanni Boccaccio undertook in the *Teseida* to compose the first martial epic in Italian (bk. 12, st. 84). He placed epic formulae of invocation at the beginning of the poem, and equally conventional addresses to his book and to the Muses at its conclusion; he imitated epic structure (the *Teseida*, like the *Aeneid* and the *Thebaid*, has twelve books) and diction, reinforcing the latter by some nearly verbatim translations from Statius. But if, in all these ways, Boccaccio self-consciously donned the epic mantle, he also brought to his encounter with Statius literary sensibilities formed by medieval courtly romance and lyric, and thereby created in the *Teseida* a new, hybrid version of the noble life. Boccaccio's eclecticism declares itself at the poem's beginning; he will tell of "the deeds of Arcita and of Palemone the good, born of royal blood, as it seems, and both Thebans; and although kinsmen, they came into conflict by their excessive love for Emilia, the beautiful Amazon" (bk. 1, st. 5, translations mine). The fate of a love affair, not a city, provides a suitably elevated subject. (Even the full title of the work is eclectic: *The Thesiad* [epic] *of Emily's Nuptials* [romance].)

The first book of the *Teseida* cleverly splices Boccaccio's story into Statius's epic world by recounting Teseo's war against the Amazons (mentioned but not described by the Roman poet) and his marriage to Ipolita. Early in the second book, Boccaccio links up with the *Thebaid*'s account of the last stages of the Theban war, and moves quickly to Teseo's encounter with the Greek widows at his triumphant homecoming from Scythia (bk. 2, st. 25). The bulk of book two recounts Teseo's triumph over Creon (whom he kills, as in Statius) and the funeral observances for the Greek warriors. Neither Argia, Antigone, nor the pyre with the twin-tongued flame appear; Teseo is at stage center throughout. Then, as a coda to the action at Thebes, the Greeks who are searching the battlefield for their dead and wounded find two young men, badly wounded and calling for death, whose demeanor and dress proclaim them to be of royal blood. The princes are taken to Teseo, who treats them with respect and holds them in comfortable detention in Athens as book two ends. Thenceforth Palemone and Arcita, the young Thebans, usurp the plot from Teseo, thanks to their love for Emilia, Ipolita's sister (and a character unknown to Statius), which transforms their friendship into a near-mortal rivalry.

The first two books of the *Teseida* abound with self-conscious references to Boccaccio's appropriation of the epic heritage for his own uses. The most obvious emblem of poetic metamorphosis is the discovery and "resurrection" of the half-dead Palemone and Arcita from the field of corpses that constitutes the end of the Theban war and the end of Statius's epic about it. In the *Thebaid,* Polynices and Eteocles "overcome" death by the sheer force of their mutual hatred, becoming, through the image of the warring flames, a symbol of destructive destiny's extension beyond the limits of any single life. Boccaccio replaces the pyre scene by the discovery scene, substituting a new beginning for epic closure, and his own heroes for Statius's. Moreover, Teseo responds to the new protagonists in a courteous, refined manner that distinguishes him from the spirit of the epic universe. When Palemone and Arcita are brought before him, he hears the *sdegno real* (royal disdain) in their voices (bk. 2, st. 89), but doesn't respond to such *ira* as it deserves. Instead he is *pio* (compassionate), heals them, and, despite their danger to his rule, refuses to kill them, as that would be a great sin (bk. 2, st. 98); as book two ends, he installs them in his palace, to be served "at their pleasure" (bk. 2, st. 99).

One more emblem of the transformation the Italian poet has wrought on his Roman master's view of the noble life deserves special mention. After Teseo defeats Ipolita in battle, he falls in love with her, and his sudden subjection to Cupid (bk. 1, sts. 129–31) is accompanied by an equally unexpected collective metamorphosis of all Ipolita's Amazon followers: as soon as they put down their arms, they revert to being paragons of beauty and grace; their stern battle cries become pleasant jests and sweet songs, and even their steps, which were great strides when they fought, are dainty once again (bk. 1, st. 132). Boccaccio was inspired to this felicitous passage by Statius's image of the domesticated Hippolyta, arriving in Athens as Theseus's captive and wife. But here a whole society of wild Scythian women spontaneously suffers a sea-change of beautifying refinement, manifesting precisely the transformation that *courtoisie* as a behavioral ideal imposed on the ruder manners of European feudal society in the centuries just prior to Boccaccio's own, and that the courtly romance and lyric imposed on the martial style of the classical and feudal epic.

In deflecting the *Thebaid* from epic into a new, mixed genre, the *Teseida* comes to grips with the epic theme of order versus chaos in new ways, such as the emphasis on control and refinement implicit in Teseo's courteous treatment of Palemone and Arcita when they are first brought to him as captives, and in the metamorphosis of Ipolita's warriors after their defeat. Control also manifests itself in other elements of the poem. Boccaccio's mastery of epic conventions—those already mentioned, plus personified prayers flying to heaven (bk. 7), catalogues of heroes arriving for battle (bk. 6), descriptions of funeral obsequies and games (bk. 11)—is a self-conscious exercise of poetic control, and the summit of literary self-consciousness is the temple Palemone builds to honor Arcita's memory: it is decorated with pictures that recapitulate the entire story of the *Teseida* (except Arcita's mortal fall from his horse!), and the narrator characterizes it as "a perfect work by one who knew how to execute it superbly" (bk. 11, st. 70)—that is, by Boccaccio himself. The fact, however, that the "perfect work" omits the one detail of its protagonist's story—his death—that has called the temple and its pictures into being suggests that perfect control in art (and life?) is an illusion, created by overlooking those situations in which chaos erupts.

A similar cynicism about control underlies the manipulative gamesmanship used from time to time by Boccaccio's characters in dealing with persons and events. Emilia, having realized that Palemone and Arcita are watching her from their prison when she plays in her garden, encourages their ardor by flirtatious behavior—but out of vanity, not love (bk. 3, sts. 8–30). Arcita, having been released from prison by Peritoo's intercession with Teseo, speaks ambiguously to his benefactors, and lies outright to his kinsman Palemone, the better to hide his passion and his plans to assuage it (bk. 3, sts. 56–76). Nor is desire the only nurse of deceit; in book nine, after Palemone and Arcita, with one hundred followers each, have fought a tournament with Emilia as the prize, Teseo consoles those on the losing side with diplomatic words, blaming the defeat on the will of Providence, and complimenting them as the best warriors he has ever seen (bk. 9, sts. 51–60). The beneficiaries of Teseo's game of diplomacy are pleased, even though they don't believe all they have heard (bk. 9, st. 61)!

The *Teseida*'s ironic view of strategies for controlling life and art ripens at times into open recognition of how attempts to defeat chaos falter when faced by its irresistible forces. When Arcita, having encountered Palemone in the woods outside Athens, attempts to dissuade him from a fight to the finish over Emilia, he recalls the wrath of the gods against the Theban lineage to which they both belong; he points out that they are victims of Fortune, and says that in any case the winner of such a battle still will not have Emilia—and then, having marshalled all these sound arguments against strife, ends with the thumping non sequitur that since Palemone wishes the battle, he shall indeed have it (bk. 5, sts. 49–60). Dominated by love's passion, Arcita can see (and speak) the truth, but cannot act on it. Later, at the climax of the story, the gods whose wrath Arcita has invoked as a reason for not fighting, intervene decisively (but not on epic grounds) when the young kinsmen commit themselves to battle for Emilia under Teseo's aegis. Arcita, who has prayed to Mars for victory, wins the tournament, only to be thrown from his horse and fatally wounded as he rides about the arena in triumph; Venus sends a Fury to startle the horse, so that she can award Emilia to Palemone, her votary. Emilia, denied her desire to remain chaste and marry neither Theban, can only blame Love for her sorry state (bk. 8, st. 96).

To the extent that the poem's characters can control their fates by manipulation, their strategies of control and deceit make them figures of irony. But when they become prisoners of larger forces, they (and the poem's rhetoric about them) become pathetic and sentimentalized. This polarity of responses between ironic comedy, when characters act artfully, and pathetic melodrama, when they suffer victimization, differs markedly from our responses to the struggle between order and chaos in book twelve of the *Thebaid*. There Theseus's championship of civilized values is intended to provoke admiration, not cynical amusement, and the furious excesses of Polynices, Eteocles, and Creon horrified repugnance, not sentimental involvement. Sometimes, in the *Teseida*, sentiment and irony seem to pervade a scene simultaneously, especially a scene conceived in terms of the literary conventions of courtly love. The hot sighs of Palemone and Arcita in prison, as they debate whether Emilia is a goddess or a woman, and then languish and grow pale with lovesickness (bk. 3, sts. 12–38), conform so completely to those conventions as to invite us to smile at the predictability of it all, even as we sympathize with the helplessness of the imprisoned lovers. Elsewhere, our compassionate response to the affection the young men frequently express for each other must battle with our sense of the absurdity implicit in the repeated spectacle of the two dear friends trying to beat each other's brains out to win Emilia.

Much more than the *Thebaid*, then, the *Teseida* moves toward an interpretive impasse, resulting from the tense equilibrium between activity and passivity, irony and pathos, in its portrayal of the issues at stake in the noble life. Only Teseo's commanding presence seems to offer a way out of this labyrinth. Except for the brief period in book one where he suffers from lovesickness for the vanquished Ipolita, Teseo is the active principle throughout the poem. He lacks the symbolic integrity of Statius's Theseus, the agent of civilization in a world driven mad with rage; rather, he functions as an emblem of controlled variousness in a world where variety of response and perception continually leads to situations of collision between and within selves. For example, when Teseo addresses the Greek widows who have sought his aid against Creon, he moves within a single stanza from being "wounded in his heart by profound pity" to speaking "in a loud voice kindled by rage" (bk. 2, st. 43). Unlike Palemone or Arcita, Teseo is not hindered by such extremes. He acts with complete martial authority, killing Creon and capturing Thebes, then responds to the wrath of the distraught, newly captured Theban princes when they are brought before him by a show of magnanimity beyond their deserts (bk. 2, st. 89); or, finding them later fighting in the woods, he not only grants them the amnesty they request for having broken his laws, but rewards them richly (bk. 5, st. 105). He presides gravely over Arcita's obsequies and then, in a triumphant show of authority, convinces Palemone and Emilia to marry, despite their deeply felt unwillingness so to sully the memory of the departed prince (bk. 12, sts. 4–43).

Teseo, in short, makes everything look easy, and in so doing, he seems less to reflect a large view of the noble life as the triumph of order over chaos than to represent within the poem the virtuosity of its creator in assimilating and combining epic and courtly romance conventions, and thus the triumph of ingenuity over disparateness. The *Teseida*'s major concerns are finally aesthetic rather than moral or philosophical; its ultimate referent is literature, not experience.

III

When Geoffrey Chaucer undertook to adapt the *Teseida* for his Knight's Tale, he performed an impressive feat of truncation, shortening Boccaccio's nearly 10,000 lines to 2,250 and compressing twelve books into four. Chaucer's omissions, and the way he has the Knight call attention to them, affect the meaning as well as the length of his revision of the *Teseida*. The change most immediately noticeable to a reader of both texts is Chaucer's wholesale jettisoning of Boccaccio's self-consciously literary epic trappings—invocations, glosses, catalogues of warriors—so that the story, as told by the Knight, sounds much less like a virtuoso performance, much more like the effort of an amateur—a soldier, not a poet—who, far from taking pride like Boccaccio in his poetic achievement, wishes primarily to finish his task as quickly as possible. (The one exception to the Knight's attitude of self-abnegation, his description of the tournament lists constructed by Theseus, will be discussed shortly.) The Knight shares his creator's desire to abridge his "auctor," although, unlike other, more learned or artistic Chaucerian narrators, he never alludes to his source either by real name (as in the reference to "Petrark" in the Clerk's Tale) or pseudonymously (the "Lollius," alias Boccaccio, of *Troilus and Criseyde*). The rhetorical device by which the Knight (and behind him, Chaucer) calls attention to the process of abridgment is *occupatio*, the deliberate refusal to amplify (or describe completely) some aspect of the narrative. The Knight's first use of *occupatio* comes only fifteen lines into his tale:

> And certes, if it nere to long to heere,
> I wolde have toold yow fully the manere
> How wonnen was the regne of Femenye

> By Theseus and by his chivalrye;
> And of the grete bataile for the nones
> Bitwixen Atthenes and Amazones;
> And how asseged was Ypolita,
> The faire, hardy queene of Scithia;
> And of the feste that was at hir weddynge,
> And of the tempest at hir hoom-comynge;
> But al that thyng I moot as now forbere.
>
> (ll. 875–85, F. N. Robinson, 2d ed.)

Chaucer here digests the first book and beginning of the second of the *Teseida* by having the Knight, in effect, tell us what he won't tell us. Chaucer included these details of his omission, not because the story as he tells it needs them, but in order to dramatize the fact that storytelling requires the constant exercise of control in selecting material from a potentially much greater reservoir—ultimately, in fact, from all experience and all antecedent literature. *Occupatio* is an emblem of the hard choices and discipline of art: what do I leave out? And the Knight, as an amateur, is particularly troubled by this aspect of his task, given the scope of his chosen story and his lack of skill. As he puts it:

> I have, God woot, a large feeld to ere,
> And wayke been the oxen in my plough.
> The remenant of the tale is long enough.
>
> (ll. 886–88)

Although the Knight's reference to his limited powers is a traditional *captatio benevolentiae,* it strikes a very different note from Boccaccio's self-confident epic invocations. The image of the oxen and plough is homely and unpretentious, and the idea it conjures up of the rest of the tale stretching before its teller like a great, untilled field conveys some of the nervous discomfort felt by the amateur who sets out to tell a story without fully controlling it, knowing that in any case his best hope is to shorten it where he can.

The Knight's difficulties in discharging his unaccustomed artistic responsibilities surface most spectacularly in his description of Arcite's funeral rites. He recounts in some detail the procession of mourners from Athens to the place of immolation (the same grove where Palamon and Arcite first fought for Emelye), and then launches into an *occupatio* forty-seven lines long (ll. 2919–66), in which he describes the rest of the obsequies (including funeral games) while protesting that he will not do so! The distension of a curtailing device to a size that completely defeats its rhetorical intent is a masterful comic stroke on Chaucer's part, but also a strategy designed to drive home the impression of the amateur poet unable to control his material.

Precariousness of control in fact constitutes a main theme of the Knight's Tale, linking the Knight's ad hoc artistic activities with the political, and finally philosophical, program of Theseus by which the Athenian duke attempts to solve the potentially disruptive problem of Palamon and Arcite. And behind Theseus lies yet a deeper level of unresolved tension: the ambivalence of the Knight about life's meaning, as revealed in his treatment of his characters. At this last, most profound level, Chaucer confronts the paradoxes inherent in chivalry, and thereby transforms Boccaccio's literary tour de force into a troubling anatomy of an archaic but, in his day, still influential ideal of the noble life.

The theme of precarious control finds emblematic embodiment in a detail included by the Knight in his description (absent in Boccaccio) of the preparations for the tournament battle between Palamon and Arcite. Amidst the bustle of knights, squires, blacksmiths, musicians, and expert spectators sizing up the combatants, he directs our attention to "the fomy stedes on the golden brydel / Gnawynge" (ll. 2506–7)—a superb image of animal passion at its most elemental, restrained by the civilizing force of the (symbolic, we feel) golden bridle, but clearly anxious to throw off restraint and liberate energy.

The golden bridle is a microcosm of the entire artifice of civilization—the officially sanctioned tournament and the lists in which it is held—with which Theseus seeks to enclose and control the love-inspired martial energy of Palamon and Arcite. The lists deserve attention as a focal point of the Knight's Tale that illustrates with special clarity Chaucer's intent in transforming the *Teseida.* Chaucer has Theseus build them especially for this battle (in Boccaccio the *teatro* where the tournament is held preexists the rivalry of Palemone and Arcita); they are thus an emblem of his authority and wisdom in dealing with the young Thebans who threaten him politically and who wish to marry his ward. Furthermore, the description of the lists constitutes the sole instance when the Knight, abandoning *occupatio,* waxes eloquent and self-confidently poetic.

The lists, therefore, fuse the high point of the Knight's art of language and Theseus's art of government.

Theseus orders the lists to be built after he interrupts Palamon and Arcite fighting viciously, up to their ankles in blood, in the woods outside Athens to decide who will have Emelye. The tournament which the lists will house, and of which Theseus will be the "evene juge . . . and trewe" (l. 1864), represents a revision of his first intention, which was to kill the young combatants when he accidentally comes upon them—one a fugitive from his prison, the other under sentence of perpetual exile from Athens—fighting on his territory without his permission: "Ye shal be deed, by myghty Mars the rede!" (l. 1747). This second, less furious response of Theseus to the love-inspired violence of his former prisoners is also a second, more legal chance for Palamon and Arcite to fight over Emelye. Theseus controls himself, and thus controls the lovers' behavior. And since the lists are built on the very spot where Theseus found Palamon and Arcite in battle (l. 1862), the imposition of the constructed edifice on the hitherto wild grove provides yet another image of civilized control, this time over nature.

The significance of the lists grows as we learn that Theseus calls together all the master craftsmen and artists of his realm to perform the work of construction (ll. 1895–1901); indeed, in the light of these facts, and of the extended description of the finished product (ll. 1887–2088), we are justified in hearing echoes of Genesis (echoes that emphasize Theseus's powers of control) in the Knight's comment ending his account: "Theseus, / That at his grete cost arrarayed thus / The temples and the theatre every deel / Whan it was doon, hym lyked wonder weel" (ll. 2089–92). But if Theseus is the deity behind this work of art and government, he must share the honors of godhead with the Knight, who not only uses the same verb, "devyse," to denominate the activities of those who made the lists (l. 1901) and his own activity in describing it (l. 1914), but also (with artistic ineptitude but, for Chaucer, thematic significance) destroys the distance between his reality and that of his tale by describing, as if he had seen them, the insides of the temples built at three compass points atop the round enclosure of the lists ("Ther saugh I . . ."; ll. 1995, 2062, 2065, etc.). Although the Knight clearly admires Theseus more than any other character throughout his tale, nowhere does he identify himself so directly with his surrogate as here, where both are constructing a universal image of their willed authority over their respective poetic and political worlds.

In the *Teseida,* we hear of the "teatro eminente," where the tournament will be held, at the beginning of book seven, but no details of its construction are given until stanzas 108–10, and then a mere twenty-four lines suffice (as opposed to Chaucer's two hundred). In between, various activities and speeches reduce the *teatro* to the periphery of our attention. Chaucer, instead, moves directly from Theseus's decision to build the lists to the elaborate description of them. He also includes in the description (and the structure) the temples to Mars, Venus, and Diana, which in the *Teseida* are not earthly but celestial edifices to which the prayers of Palemone, Arcita, and Emilia ascend. The cumulative effect of Chaucer's compression and redistribution of Boccaccian detail is to make of the lists the poem's dominant image, and a true *theatrum mundi*: an image of the universe, with men below and gods above (the temples are located above the gates or in a turret; ll. 1903–9), and Theseus in the middle, imposing order and public legitimacy on the private passions of Palamon and Arcite.

Seen in this light, the lists are also a concrete, palpable version and foreshadowing of the cosmic order, held together by Jupiter's "cheyne of love" (l. 2988), which Theseus invokes in his last act of control, his proposal and arrangement of a marriage between Palamon and Emelye some years after Arcite's death. And, because of the self-consciousness of the Knight about his artistry, the lists also claim a place in the cosmic order for poetry—not Boccaccio's epic-revival art, with its purely literary and aesthetic triumphalism, but a socially useful poetry that reflects and promotes cosmic order in a manner analogous to the deeds of a good governor. The close relationship between the enterprises of Theseus and the Knight is suggested by the direct juxtaposition of the passage expressing the duke's godlike satisfaction in his creation and this other judgment on the quality of the painting (i.e., of the poetic description) in the temples: "Wel koude he peynten lifly that it wroghte; / With many a floryn he the hewes boghte" (ll. 2087–88).

The mention of the costs attendant upon the artist's triumph provides a transition to the larger costs of the ordering activities undertaken by Theseus. First of all, the gods Mars, Venus, and Diana are presented by Chaucer as much more threatening to human happiness than their Boccaccian equivalents, thanks to the later poet's insertion into the temple ecphrases of an accumulation of details illustrating catastrophic divine intervention in human life (ll. 1995–2023, 2056–72, etc.). More crucially, Chaucer invents the figure of Saturn, grandfather of Venus and Mars and presiding deity over the greatest human disasters, who undertakes to solve the problem created by his grandchildren's respective partisanship for Palamon and Arcite: Venus has promised to answer Palamon's prayer for Emelye, Mars Arcite's for victory. Theseus, acting as patron of the Theban princes, calls the lists into being, but the last word belongs to Saturn, who undertakes to use Theseus's creation to assert his own patronage over the celestial counterparts of Palamon and Arcite. Hence the question arises: has Theseus's activity, culminating in the building of the lists, really imposed order on potentially disruptive passions of love and prowess, or has it merely provided a compact and intensified "inner circle" within which the passions—and the uncontrollable divine destiny that sponsors them—can operate to intensify human misery?

This is a sobering question, and not, I believe, one that can easily be answered positively or negatively from the data given us by the Knight's Tale, albeit many critics have tried, over the years, to argue for Chaucer's philosophical optimism (or more rarely, pessimism) on the basis of the tale. It seems to me more useful to search out the source of this deep ambivalence about human happiness—about whether the golden bridle and the lists control human violence or merely license and intensify it—and thereby to understand more clearly the poet's intent in creating the Knight's Tale. And here, in my view, is where the fact that the tale is told by a professional warrior becomes extremely important.

Chaucer establishes the Knight's professional perspective on the tale he tells—and on life itself—in several passages, too frequently ignored by critics, describing events and feelings directly related to the career of a practitioner of martial chivalry. One such passage I have already mentioned: the powerfully mimetic description of the preparations for the tournament (ll. 2491–2522), rich with the closely observed sights and sounds of the stable, the grounds, and even the palace, where would-be experts, like bettors at a race track, choose their favorites in the coming contest:

> Somme helden with hym with the blake berd,
> Somme with the balled, some with the thikke herd;

Somme seyde, he looked grymme, and he wolde fighte.

(ll. 2517–19)

In another passage, the Knight describes the various choices of weaponry made by the participants, and ends his catalogue with the purely professional, almost bored comment: "Ther is no newe gyse [of weapon] that it nas old" (l. 2125).

The Knight's treatment of the aftermath of the tournament is as professional (almost disturbingly so) in its tone as it is amateurish in its distortion of the narrative line of his tale. When Arcite is thrown from his horse while parading around the lists in apparent triumph, the Knight immediately declares (as Boccaccio's narrator does not) that this is a critical wound; Arcite is borne to bed, "alwey criynge after Emelye" (l. 2699). The picture is infinitely pathetic: the tournament's victor pleads, as if to the heavens, for the prize he should now be enjoying, were it not for their intervention to deny it to him just when it seemed in his grasp. At this point, the Knight abruptly forsakes his wounded protagonist (and the story line) to describe in detail how Theseus entertained the rest of the tournament contestants, minimizing Arcite's injury—"he nolde noght disconforten hem alle" (l. 2704)—and assuring them that there have been no real losers on this occasion: after all, "fallyng [as Arcite did] nys nat but an aventure," and to be captured (as Palamon was) by twenty men cannot be accounted cowardice or "vileynye" (ll. 2722–30). Theseus seeks to head off "alle rancour and envye" that might lead to post-tournament disruptions of the peace (ll. 2731–34), of a kind that the Knight would have seen often enough at tournaments in his day: the duke calms the feelings of the warriors and holds a feast for them, then leads them out of town. The Knight reports Theseus's diplomacy here with the quiet approval of one who has himself been so entertained after numerous melees, and therefore recognizes how the duke has effectively defused a potentially dangerous situation—yet another instance of his ability to control life. (By contrast, the purely rhetorical performance of Teseo at the analogous point in the *Teseida* [bk. 9, sts. 51–60] is, as we have seen, greeted with some skepticism by its recipients; moreover, Boccaccio's version entirely lacks the verisimilar, "locker room" details of the combatants treating their wounds and talking about the fight after it is over—details that underscore the Knight's familiarity with the scene he is describing [ll. 2705–14].)

The Knight's professional perspective also endows the tournament fighting with a dimension of mimetic power foreign to Boccaccio. The alliterative vigor with which the combat unfolds (ll. 2601–16) and the brilliant description of Palamon's capture, despite the fury of his resistance, owing to sheer force of numbers (ll. 2636–51), convince us that a soldier is letting us see the martial life through his eyes, not (as in the *Teseida*) through the eyes of a poet steeped in epic conventions. But our deepest penetration into the Knight's vocational psyche comes, not in the lists, but when Palamon and Arcite are preparing to fight in the woods for the right to woo Emelye. Arcite, who has gone to Athens for two suits of armor, returns:

> And on his horse, allone as he was born,
> He carieth all the harneys him biforn.
> And in the grove, at tyme and place yset,
> This Arcite and this Palamon ben met.
> Tho chaungen gan the colour in hir face,
> Right as the hunters in the regne of Trace,
> That stondeth at the gappe with a spere,
> Whan hunted is the leon or the bere,
> And hereth hym come russhyng in the greves,
> And breketh both the bowes and the leves,
> And thynketh, "Heere cometh my mortal enemy!
> Withoute faille, he moot be deed, or I;
> For outher I moot sleen hym at the gappe,
> Or he moot sleen me, if that me myshappe";
> So ferden they in chaungyng of hir hewe.
>
> (ll. 1633–47)

The Knight evokes a Hemingwayesque moment of truth to describe what it feels like to be about to undertake a "mortal bataille"—an experience the General Prologue of the *Canterbury Tales* tells us he has had fifteen times. The loneliness of the moment of truth is stressed at the beginning of this passage, and the role of Fortune ("myshappe") at its conclusion. The chilling insight and particular details of this passage are entirely the Knight's (and Chaucer's), yet it has a Boccaccian point of departure, comparison with which makes Chaucer's skill and his interests even more obvious. In *Teseida* bk. 7, when Palemone and Arcita arrive at the *teatro* on the day of the tournament, each with his hundred followers, Boccaccio sums up the feelings on hearing each other's party and the roar of the crowd by using the simile of the hunter waiting for the lion. But the effect is deflating, not exalting: the hunter is so afraid, he wishes he had not spread his snares; as he waits, he wavers between being more and less terrified (bk. 7, sts. 105–7). So the young princes, facing their moment of truth, think better of their daring: "within their hearts they suddenly felt their desire become less heated" (bk. 7, st. 107). From this cynical, comic moment, Chaucer fabricates a perception of the teeth-gritting readiness for death that the professional warrior must take with him into battle.

With this moment, we plumb the absolute depths of the Knight's vision of life as a deadly, and arbitrary, business. This sense underlies another wonderfully apt remark he makes just before the escaped Palamon discovers the disguised Arcite in the grove outside Athens:

> No thyng ne knew he that it was Arcite;
> God woot he wolde have trowed it ful lite.
> But sooth is seyd, go sithen many yeres,
> That "feeld hath eyen and the wode hath eres."
> It is ful fair a man to bere hym evene,
> For al day meeteth men at unset stevene.
>
> (ll. 1519–24)

Fortune, that is, will bring together men without an appointment, and the result may well be, as it is this time, that a fight will result. The warrior must live with one hand on the hilt of his sword; he cannot expect ample warning about when to use it.

This fatalistic sense of life, quite amoral in its recognition of the uncontrollable element in human affairs, seems to me to lead the Knight toward two contrary sets of conclusions, reflected in his tale's ambivalence about the possibility of order in the world. First, by stressing the arbitrariness of events, he succeeds in reducing all of his protagonists except Theseus to the level of playthings of large forces they cannot control. Palamon and Arcite are found by *pilours*, pillagers, in a heap of dead bodies on the field outside Thebes. "Out of the taas the pilours han hem torn" (l. 1020), and this wrenching, almost Caesarean "birth" of the young heroes into the story, so different in tone from the courteous rescue afforded them by Teseo's men at this point in the *Teseida*, gives way inside three lines of verse to Theseus's decision to send them "to Atthenes, to dwellen in prisoun, / Perpetuelly" in a tower (ll. 1022–32). The import of this brusque movement from *taas* to *tour,* with all Boccaccio's intervening civilities ruthlessly extirpated, is inescapable: life is a prison into which we are born as Fortune's minions. From this point of view, the rest of Palamon's and Arcite's life is a passage in and out of prison, with the differences between captivity and liberation so blurred that at one point Arcite can call his release from the tower through the intervention of Perotheus a sentence "to dwelle / Noght in purgatorie, but in helle" (ll. 1225–26), while prison, instead, is "paradys" (l. 1237). Furthermore, the subsequent enclosures prepared for them by Theseus seem as imprisoning as the tower; even the lists, in this reading, render the young princes helpless before Saturn's whim, which is as arbitrary as Theseus's initial decision to imprison them, but more deadly. When Arcite is thrown from his horse, he is "korven out of his harneys" (l. 2696) and carried off to die—a grim act of release that recalls his being torn out of the *taas,* and supports a dark view of life as a succession of equally brutal operations of imprisonment and release performed upon humanity by an indifferent or hostile universe.

The Knight, when he espouses this dark view, becomes practically as heedless of the feelings of his characters as is Saturn. He makes fun of the young lovers, and turns their heartfelt, Boethian complaints about the meaning of this cruel life into a *dubbio,* or love-problem game, at the end of part one. He leers at Emelye as she performs her rites of purification before praying to Diana to remain a virgin (a prayer doomed to rejection; ll. 2282–88), and, as we have seen, he leaves the wounded Arcite crying for Emelye while he recapitulates Theseus's diplomatic treatment of the rest of the tournament combatants. We are surely intended by Chaucer to blanch in horror at the grim levity with which the Knight ends his expert description of Arcite's mortal condition:

> Nature hath now no dominacioun,
> And certeinly, ther Nature wol not wirche,
> Fare wel physik! go ber the man to chirche!
>
> (ll. 2758–60)

It is against this strand of professionally inspired pessimism and stoicism that the image of Theseus the bringer of order must be placed—as the mouthpiece of a philosophical optimism that expresses the Knight's pulling back from the edge of the abyss to which his sense of death and fortune leads him. Like Statius so many centuries before him, the Knight needs Theseus, and at the ending of his tale allows Theseus's last diplomatic initiative complete success. Invoking the order of the universe to explain to the still grief-stricken Palamon and Emelye why they should no longer mourn for Arcite, Theseus counsels them "to maken vertu of necessitee," and "make of sorwes two / O parfit joye, lastynge everemo" by marrying (ll. 3042, 3071–72). The rhetoric here is at least in part Boethian—with, as critics have noted, some odd turns—but the strategy behind it is wholly political. Theseus has been led to propose the marriage by his desire "to have with certeyn countrees alliaunce, / And have fully of Thebans obeisaunce" (ll. 2973–74). For him, this is a dynastic alliance, and thus another imposition of political order on human passions (here, grief). Because the Knight has given vent to his darker perceptions elsewhere in his tale, however, we are allowed, nay, intended to take some of Theseus's philosophic justifications for his political initiative *cum grano salis*. We know by now how precarious and potentially ironic the duke's structures of control can be, even if the Knight wishes to forget this. Indeed, even here, the phrases from Theseus's speech about virtue and necessity, sorrow and joy, encourage us to detect someone's desperation—whether Theseus's or the Knight's is not clear—to find an alternative to the dark despair that flooded the poem with Arcite's death. The lingering influence of that despair inheres in Theseus's reference to "this foule prisoun of this lyf" (l. 3061), a phrase ironically recalling the tower to which he condemned Palamon and Arcite early in the story, thus literally making their life a prison.

The secret of Chaucer's recreation of the *Teseida* as the Knight's Tale lies, then, in his vivid and profound comprehension of the tensions that might well exist within the *Weltanschauung* of a late medieval mercenary warrior. Or perhaps he simply appreciated the contradictions in his society's concept of chivalry. The knight of Chaucer's day carried with him a very mixed baggage of Christian idealism, archaic and escapist codes of conduct, aesthetically attractive routines of pageantry, and a special function as the repository of skills and graces appropriate to the training of young aristocrats. In his famous General Prologue portrait, Chaucer's own knight possesses a high moral character of an archaic (if not totally imaginary) kind: "fro the time that he first began / To riden out, he loved chivalrie, / Trouthe and honour, freedom and curteisie" (ll. 44–46). He combines this idealism of outlook and behavior ("he nevere yet no vileynie ne sayde / In al his lyf unto no maner wight," ll. 70–71) with a thoroughly professional mercenary career that has taken him to most of the places where the noble warrior's virtues and skills could be practiced during Chaucer's day. This synthetic phenomenon, the idealistic killer (he had "foughten for oure feith at Tramyssene / In lystes thries, and ay slayn his foo," ll. 62–63), embodies in his person some but not all of the main strands of chivalry. His son, the Squire who accompanies him on the pilgrimage, supplements these by personifying the virtuosic and aesthetic side of late medieval chivalry: he sings, dances, loves hotly, and fights very little. Chaucer's splitting of the chivalric complex into two generationally distinct segments allowed him to isolate what seemed to him the real paradox of chivalry—its imposition of moral idealism on a deadly, and therefore potentially nihilistic, profession—for treatment in the Knight's Tale, leaving its decorative aspects to be teased in the harmlessly inept story told (but not completed) by the Squire, himself an unfinished creature, when his turn comes on the road to Canterbury.

The Knight's Tale, reflecting as it does the problematic view of life implicit in a code that seeks to moralize and dignify aggression, looks back across the centuries to enter into dialogue with the last book of Statius's *Thebaid*, as well as with Boccaccio's *Teseida*, on the question of what Charles Muscatine calls "the struggle between noble designs and chaos." Reading Chaucer's chivalric tale with its ancestry in mind heightens our appreciation of both the uniqueness of his art and the continuities of its tradition.

Sic et Non: Discarded Worlds in the Knight's Tale

F. Anne Payne

That the Knight's Tale, a philosophical parody with *The Consolation* [*of Philosophy*] and the romance as its models, belongs to the serio-comic tradition of Menippean satire is abundantly evident in much of the critical literature that surrounds the poem. While it has never, to my knowledge, had its particular and peculiar elements explained by being related to this genre, the traits characteristic of the satire are commented on frequently. That the tale is a parody of its ostensible genre, the romance, has been recognized and the presence of the inserted text, the *Consolation,* clearly documented; the multiplicity of tones and voices, often illustrated; the presence of unreconciled oppositions and the difficulty of determining the poem's meaning, frequently observed. The subject of order—the organization that Menippean satire sees men trying to impose on chaos with their theories, explanations, and structures—is central to the tale and also to the critical debate that surrounds it.

Yet, in spite of this help, the implications and directions that Chaucer gives to Menippean conventions in the Knight's Tale are more complex to interpret than those of either *Troilus* or the Nun's Priest's Tale. With *Troilus,* once the subcategory in Menippean satire, Menippean tragedy, is recognized, the poem becomes susceptible of interpretation. The Nun's Priest's Tale propounds a difficult "who am I" riddle, but like all riddles, contains a toughness that holds up until the answer is found. In the Knight's Tale, however, the pursuit of what seem to be promising interlinking conventions and ideas usually ends in our being turned out into the cold, very gently, but turned out nevertheless. The tale is not a Menippean tragedy like *Troilus* (or any other kind of tragedy, though it flirts continually with tragic issues). Nor does it propound a riddle, as does the Nun's Priest's Tale. It lacks the free laughter of Menippean comedy such as we find in Lucian, Boethius, and perhaps even the Nun's Priest's Tale (though laughing with the devil eventually provides an unendurable strain on our capacity for amusement).

The Menippean dialogue in the Knight's Tale is easily visible and so is the textual parody; certainly for identifying the genre of the tale as Menippean satire, both are important. The dialogue, with Theseus (the counterpart of Philosophy) and Palamon and Arcite (the counterparts of Boethius), takes as its subject the controlling question of the tale, which knight shall have the lady. Palamon and Arcite struggle for ten years to find a method of resolving their conflict over Emily. The *deus* figures—Saturn, Mars, and Venus—preside over the solution directly. Theseus, who gives the knights' emotional desire a constructive outlet, builds lists, arranges a tournament, and finally convenes a parliament to resolve the issue. The textual parody, created by the large injection into the formal story of serious philosophical issues reminiscent of those raised by Boethius, is constantly before us. The juxtaposition of a lightweight problem from romance and profound philosophical questioning sets up the familiar dialogical milieu of Menippean satire. Yet those common parodic devices become almost immediately, in any insistent thinking about the poem, only parts of a larger satiric interest.

When we compare the tale with more complex issues in Menippean satire, we find that Chaucer adds a dimension of ironic observation, which, for the task of interpreting the tale, has the force and effect of the proverbial monkey wrench. For instance, the juxtaposition of characters with unmatched problems, espousing opposing philosophies of life, whose positions we are required to examine, is a commonplace in Menippean satire, a primary method of filling up its foreground and of portraying its basic assumption, namely that the reality of things is "out there" but unknowable, that there is, therefore, no accurate standard, no recognized true answer, which mortals can use to guide their lives and assess their thinking. Hence, in some desperate and paradoxical sense, which it generally elects to treat as comic, it proposes that if it is our nature to spend our time energetically preparing for this search, there is nevertheless nothing to be found by going out there to look. To counteract this nothingness, the satirists direct our attention to intellectual confrontations, to multivoiced conflicts drawn from the various representations in the spheres of human knowledge. The satirist keeps us, verbally at least, in the midst of this chaos by not bringing to the forefront his own resolutions to the incipient clash between his various theoretical and mythical formulations. When the conflict threatens, he offers us pauses and right-angle turns. Both occur because of new events in the story or because of new decisions of characters who have egos power-ful enough or are lucky enough to impose their will momentarily on the minds of those with whom they deal. Because of their unexpectedness, these changes of pace and direction allow brief moments of freedom from the conflict, but they disappear as we adjust to the new tempos. They allow us to hope for a while before we discover that the old problem is still there and the new beginning offers no truthful insight into the complexity of things.

Chaucer's innovation in the Knight's Tale is that, in addition to juxtaposing sharply opposed, never reconciled views of the world, he batters and undermines us with the implication that neither oppositions nor possible reconciliations are of any great conse-quence to the Knight. By a variety of means, Chaucer blurs the focus of the oppositions, ignores or siphons off the energy the active reader commonly dedicates to resolving them, and thus keeps us in the constant experience of anticlimax and abandonment. With this extra dimension, the tale is, in fact, a brilliant tour de force, a parody of the energetic interest which Menippean satire dedicates to its dialogical conflicts.

A minor example of what happens on scales large and small in the tale is found in the *demande d'amour* passage that ends part 1. Arcite, released by Pirithous, has left Athens; Palamon is still im-prisoned. Both have uttered their Boethian complaints, Arcite about happiness (ll. 1223–74, F. N. Robinson, 2d ed.), Palamon about justice (ll. 1303–33). The Knight at this point requests that we pause and consider:

> Yow loveres axe I now this questioun:
> Who hath the worse, Arcite or Palamoun?
>
> (ll. 1347–48)

He goes on to pursue the facets of the dilemma with the opposing questions, Is it better to see what you want everyday, but be bound in such a way as to be incapable of approaching it? or, Is it better to be free to do whatever you like, but excluded from the sight of what you want? The problem is not without interest; various metaphoric applications spring to mind. But the point is that the narrator deserts us and the dilemma at once to move on in response to unexplained demands, which, since we cannot grasp them, leave us feeling orphaned.

> Now demeth as yow liste, ye that kan,
> For I wol telle forth as I began.
>
> (ll. 1353–54)

What is done on a small scale in the *demande d'amour* passage is done on the largest scales in the poem. A major conflict which turns up again and again—treated, it is true, as if it had no deep import, no power to clarify anything about the problems of the universe we exist in—is the conflict between "love's law" and "positive law," Arcite's names for two opposing world views. Arguing with unconscious profundity, he justifies his right to love Emily by saying early in the poem:

> "Love is a gretter lawe, by my pan
> Than may be yeve to any erthely man;
> And therfore positif lawe and swich decree
> Is broken al day for love in ech degree."
>
> (ll. 1165–68)

Positive law is, according to Robinson, "a technical term. 'Lex positiva,' as opposed to natural law, is that which rests solely upon man's decree." (For instance: If I see her first, she's mine.)

The distinction that Arcite makes recalls the passage in the *Romance of the Rose,* where Reason proves to the lover that Love is superior to Justice. Justice, she tells him, ruled at the time of Saturn. But when his son, Jupiter, castrated him and Venus was born in the sea foam from his severed genitals, she departed. If this Justice of the Saturnalian Age were to return to earth now, it would, unless men loved one another, cause great destruction. But if men loved as before, "everyone in the world would then live peacefully and tranquilly, and they would never have a king or prince; there would be neither bailiff nor provost as long as people lived honestly. Judges would never hear any clamor. So I say that Love by itself is worth more than Justice, even though the latter works against Malice" (l. 5555ff., trans. Charles Dahlberg). The justice of the Olympian Age is little more than positive law. The opposition that Arcite names hints at larger categories of opposition: Golden Age and Iron Age, old gods and new gods, matriarchy and patriarchy—oppositions which all, in their way, appear in the Knight's Tale.

Positive law accounts for codes of agreement in the poem—for example, for the codes of brothers, knights, and national alliances. Its high values are legal justice and political—if need be, martial—order. Its gods are the Olympians, with Jupiter as king. In contrast to this world is the world of natural law, within whose scope in the poem fall Emily, beauty, love, happiness. It is a world without rules in a legal or categorical sense, a world which men perceive darkly, but nevertheless, a world which inspires even despair with meaning. Its gods are the gods of the old order, Saturn and his last self-engendered child, Venus. Natural law is the law of the culture that Brewer designates "unofficial" (the culture of women), and positive law, the law of "official culture" (the culture of men). The two are distinguished, he points out, in that unofficial culture wants quick benefits, the joys and delights of the moment, while official culture would extend all benefits until death. The Knight and other Menippean satirists think that it is our fate, male and female, to be able to look at conventional codifications of excluding oppositions and enjoy the benefits and burdens of either side, and perhaps, most joyous of all, be wary enough of truth to see the oppositions as inconsequential, even if amusingly attractive.

Although the outlines of these oppositions are blurred in the tale, they are nevertheless relatively easy to see. The laws or worlds providing the terms of the conflict exist on the private and public levels and are reflected in the heavens when the gods' activities catch fire from the desires of the knights and Emily. The components of these two laws and the worlds they govern set up a number of antitheses which the poem can be said to explore dismissively: beauty and brotherhood (the private problem), love and order (the public problem), happiness and justice (the divine problem). The contrast, conflict, and philosophical interactions of the planes on which the laws operate, planes which seem to intersect only because the same mind is capable of considering both (not because the Knight proposes any kind of strong and deliberate contest between them), are to be discovered in whatever phase of the text we care to consider. The presence of the opposition is perhaps most evident in the knights' attempt to find a way between the dictates of the beauty of Emily and the code of their sworn brotherhood. For this particular confrontation, Arcite's terms for the two laws (love's law and positive law) could suffice, but I have also used the term "natural law" as synonymous with "love's law."

The tale's foreground focuses on the knights' struggle with one another; complicating their problem is each one's inner struggle to relate this new perception to the vision of life he had before. In all phases of their relation to the goal represented by Emily, their attitudes differ radically and consistently. In the first part of their private ordeal, which takes place in prison, each becomes identified with one of the two systems: Palamon with love's law and Arcite with positive law. Palamon, mistaking Emily for Venus, chief goddess of the realm of love, says: "Venus, if it be thy wil / Yow in this gardyn thus to transfigure / Bifore me, sorweful, wrecched creature, / Out of this prisoun help that we may scapen" (ll. 1104–7). Arcite, identifying Emily as a beautiful woman, allies himself with positive law. He says accurately to Palamon: "Thyn is affeccioun of hoolynesse, / And myn is love, as to a creature" (ll. 1158–59). Their preferences are apparent also in their naming of the god who ruins their lives. Palamon, in his complaint at the end of part 1, names the Titan Saturn as one of the gods whose jealousy places him in prison, and he blames Venus, too, for his unhappiness:

> "But I moot been in prisoun thurgh Saturne,
> And eek thurgh Juno, jalous and eek wood,
> That hath destroyed wel ny al the blood
> Of Thebes with his waste walles wyde;
> And Venus sleeth me on that oother syde
> For jalousie and fere of hym Arcite."
>
> (ll. 1328–33)

Arcite, alone in the grove, invokes the Olympian Mars as one of the two gods whose malice keeps him enthralled: "Allas, thou felle

Mars! allas, Juno! / Thus hath youre ire oure lynage al fordo" (ll. 1559–60).

But when the knights begin to argue with one another, each adduces the other's law as grounds for giving up Emily. Palamon, in arguing priorities, cites the oaths and codes of sworn brotherhood and tries to persuade Arcite that his actions should be guided by the rules of positive law.

> This Palamon gan knytte his browes tweye.
> "It nere," quod he, "to thee no greet honour
> For to be fals, ne for to be traitour
> To me, that am thy cosyn and thy brother
> Ysworn ful depe, and ech of us til oother,
> That nevere, for to dyen in the peyne,
> Til that the deeth departe shal us tweyne,
> Neither of us in love to hyndre oother,
>
> .   .   .   .
>
> This was thyn ooth, and myn also, certeyn."
>
> (ll. 1128–39)

Arcite, on the contrary, in the passage quoted earlier (l. 1165ff.), maintains to Palamon that the law of love preempts any imaginable man-made law. He attempts to persuade Palamon that his actions should be guided by the recognition that this new experience voids all previous commitments under positive law. In this first stage of their private ordeal, the language of their arguments is dictated purely by the desire to be rid of an opponent. But that they have effectively confused themselves by the use of language not native to them is apparent in the second stage of their private ordeal, where they continue to follow the values of the law opposite to their innate inclinations.

On the one hand, Arcite, the representative of positive law, allies himself to natural law by returning to Athens after his release, thus breaking his knightly oath to Theseus and risking death (l. 1394ff.). He dedicates himself helplessly and hopelessly to the adoration of Emily in Thebes and later in Athens. In the same palace with her and, we must imagine, frequently in the same room, he regards her as a distant star whom he can see but not approach. Palamon, on the other hand, to whom this sort of adoration would be practically more appropriate, since in prison he is separated from Emily in such a way as to be able to draw no attention to himself, can think only of the war of positive law as a way to win her. (War, if won, under the terms of positive law compels assent.) He immediately assumes that Arcite, upon his release, will collect an army to obtain her (l. 1285ff.). He himself escapes from prison with the intent to do just that (l. 1483ff.). At their confrontation in the grove, their reiteration of their respective attitudes confirms their confused and individually unnatural allegiances. Palamon, acting as if he holds positive law supreme, charges Arcite with treachery to him: "And art my blood, and to my conseil sworn" (l. 1583); and then to Theseus: "And hast byjaped heere duc Theseus, / And falsly chaunged hast thy name thus!" (ll. 1585–86). Arcite, acting as if he holds natural law supreme, defies the bond between them and continues: "What, verray fool, thynk wel that love is free" (l. 1606).

The public stage of their experience and their return to their native frames of reference are initiated by the appearance at the grove of Theseus and Emily, the turning point in the action. The knights, in the encounter with this sterling representative of positive law, Theseus and his order, are released from their hopeless fight with one another into channels where they can constructively explore the way to obtaining Emily. With less trouble than Philosophy, Theseus persuades his charges to return to their abandoned methods of thought. For Palamon, Theseus's proposal removes the necessity of a war to attain Emily, and he can think how to propitiate the necessary gods. He turns once more to the world of natural law. His accompanying king is associated with Saturn, god of the Golden Age, timelessness, and hence the matriarchal system and natural law. In the temple, praying to Venus, he asks for Emily (as an Amazon representative of matriarchal values). Arcite turns back to the world of the Olympians (positive law). The king he chooses is associated with Mars, an Olympian, god of the Age of Iron, and god of war, a major occupation of the patriarchal system and positive law. In the temple, he prays to Mars and asks for victory (being winner is a central concern of patriarchal values).

That this contrast between the knights and the force of the opposing values they represent is muted by Chaucer to the point of near invisibility is evident in the energetic debate of a whole subcategory of Knight's Tale criticism: the argument about whether the knights have characteristics distinguishing them from each other. One reason for the disconcerting flattening of the issue is that no one in the tale pays any attention to the profound nature of their differences. Emily has no preference. She prays first to Diana that she not be obliged to marry either of them and then disinterestedly for the one who desires her most, as if hoping that at least the gods can make some distinction between them. For Theseus, they are young, Theban, and in love. Another reason is that they themselves switch allegiance from one law to the other for a time, an alteration which blocks and balances the consistent symbolic impression they would otherwise make. Furthermore, the Knight, who bears the intermediate responsibility for flattening the contrast, does so by lumping the knights together rhetorically as if they were always the same, playing semimythic roles of identical quality and minor significance: hero, prisoner, lover, aspirant, loser. Though Palamon wins Emily, the Knight, in what Elizabeth Salter calls the "bland denouement of the final twenty lines," fails to celebrate his success in a pointed way. He treats them offhandedly, as if their differences had no deep meaning, no power to clarify anything about the desperate struggles of men in the universe he proposes. In their presentation, Chaucer evokes profound mythic conflicts and symbols but also, by the means just suggested, discards them.

Theseus, chief representative in the public sphere of the evoked and discarded "mythic *disputatio*" of the Knight's Tale, is the most respectable of the parodies of Philosophy in Chaucer's poetry. Significant traits he possesses in common with Philosophy are the objective insight which lets him handle, untouched by doubt, the problem he presides over, a willingness to engage himself in courteous dialogue with those whose views escape his understanding, and the impulse to scoff at world views that do not coincide with his own. The latter is especially apparent in the speech where he laughs at Palamon and Arcite for fighting to the death over a woman who knows nothing of their existence, much less of their love:

> "Who may been a fool, but if he love?
> Bihoold, for Goddes sake that sit above,
> Se how they blede! be they noght wel arrayed?
> Thus hath hir lord, the god of love, ypayed
> Hir wages and hir fees for hir servyse!
> And yet they wenen for to been ful wyse
> That serven love, for aught that may bifalle.
> But this is yet the beste game of alle,

> That she for whom they han this jolitee
> Kan hem therfore as muche thank as me.
> She woot namoore of al this hoote fare,
> By God, than woot a cokkow or an hare!"
>
> (ll. 1799–1810)

Needless to say, his cynical good humor implies a level of perception totally different from the knights'.

Theseus, as is common to the Philosophy figure, is associated with positive law and is, in fact, its champion in the tale. His almost superhuman status as the advocate of the laws of man is evident in the two allusions to events from his mythic past: he fought for the rule of light and reason in Athens by killing the monster-man, the minotaur (ll. 980ff.), and for human life by rescuing Pirithous from the gods of death in the underworld (l. 1198ff.). In the events of the tale proper, he appears in the role of mediator, a balancer of the scales; at an abstract level, he is the symbol of the kind of power which makes human law inspiring. In the opening lines, we have a much-abbreviated account of his wars with the Amazons and Thebes. The Amazons are traditionally associated with the values of the matriarchal system, which is the social system of natural law; the Thebans, with the patriarchal system, which is the social system of positive law. Neither group, in myth, is absolutely confined to its system: the Amazons are fond of war, which falls in the province of positive law; the Thebans are periodically persuaded that their positive law is not synonymous with natural law (Antigone and Tiresias).

In the Knight's Tale, Theseus acts as mediator in both wars: he marries the Amazonian Hippolyte and kills the Theban Creon, thus accurately acceding to the central tenet of each (peacefully consummated love and primitive vengeance). At the end of the tale, he again symbolically resolves the conflict by marrying off the Theban Palamon to the Amazonian Emily, thus showing at least a political preference for the peaceful solutions of natural law. His resolutions are pragmatic rather than profound, but they lead to acceptable ends. For one thing, when positive law allows love to be the cause of marriage, and natural law endures the bondage of marriage's legal contract, there exists one of the few illusions of happiness which simple social man is capable of holding. For another, while Theseus's decisions do not settle the basic and all-pervasive differences between the laws, his preference for marriage as a resolution at least fits into his aims of political order without war.

In the main story, Theseus acts as mediator in the knights' longings for Emily. His tourney is the perfect example of his political mediation. Its ostensible purpose is to help the knights compete for the right to touch the world of love and beauty, but in the words which introduce the tourney, Theseus does not bother to mention the stakes (nor for that matter does the Knight). The goal of the tourney is left as the private affair of the young. The tourney, for Theseus, is a ceremonial and political occasion which, on the one hand, allows him to show the world his wealth and magnificence and, on the other hand, and much more important, allows him to fulfill an underlying political purpose. As long as he keeps the energies of the heirs of the throne of Thebes directed at each other, they do not fight him, the proper target for their warlike instincts. The tourney itself is the perfect fulfillment of Theseus's aims. The tale makes abundantly apparent that his two tactics in establishing political order are war and alliance. The tourney is a mock war; it will result in an alliance with Thebes.

But other evidence makes it clear that for all his acts of creating order anew, for all the indications that he achieves the summits human law is capable of reaching, he has no accurate understanding of or feeling for natural law. Only as long as women's presence and requests intrude upon his activities, is he both just and merciful. With chivalric good humor, he marries the Amazonian queen he had merely set out to punish for her treatment of men, as we know from the *Teseida*. At the sorrowful pleas of the women in black, he defeats the too-masculine Thebes and regains for the women the right to bury their dead. He spares the bloody knights in the grove at the ladies' request. He thinks to say in his final remark to Emily before her betrothal: "Gentil mercy oghte to passen right" (l. 3089). When he is in touch with women, in other words, pity runs soon in his gentle heart. His seeming understanding, however, is only a good-natured tolerance of the world of love's chief symbol: woman.

Without women's presence, Theseus, acting purely on his rights, imprisons the two young knights of Thebes forever. After Palamon's explanation in the grove, he condemns both knights to death to maintain his political order. And in this same episode, after pity has replaced his anger, he is still unable to see that Emily represents anything more significant than his baby sister-in-law. He sets her as the stock reward of a tournament he proposes on the spur of the moment without even the most elementary notion that her humanity requires that he secure her permission. His insensitivity is caused simply by his middle-aged (as some would have it) or male chauvinist's (as woman's liberation would have it) inability to feel or imagine the symbolic appeal of beauty. He takes the knights' violations of his laws seriously, but their love for Emily excites only his heartfelt laughter. In the latter instance, the structure of the tale forces the reader to view the love in both terms, now ludicrous, now the cause of the bittersweet paradox, wretchedness and aspiration. (The Knight, as usual, remains distant from both views of love.) Theseus's inability to understand makes him a prime example in romance literature of conventional knightly virtue. He has mastered the art of chivalric courtesy—or, in his role as the Philosophy of the Menippean structure underlying the tale, of Menippean courtesy, the art of taking other people's views into account—without going to the trouble of considering them.

We might feel that this irony directed against Theseus is so far no more deadly than that directed against Menippus and Philosophy, that Chaucer's treatment of him makes the constant point of Menippean satire that no answer or position, no matter how authoritative it may seem, can ever provide certainty. Conventionally, this figure in the satires never understands the joys which belong to time and the moment. Menippus, in the *Dialogues of the Dead,* stares at the skull of Helen and questions whether *this*, after all, was worth what was paid for it. Hermes says gently to him, reminding us, at any rate, of the values of the world of time and beauty: "Ah, but you never saw the woman alive, Menippus, or you would have said yourself that it was forgivable that they 'for such a lady long should suffer woe.' For if one sees flowers that are dried up and faded, they will, of course, appear ugly; but when they are in bloom and have their colour, they are very beautiful" (trans. M. D. Macleod). But in the Knight's Tale, Theseus is subjected to something more than the conventional irony. He is diminished, put to one side in a way that Philosophy and Menippus are not. The effect of this treatment is to make him and his powers as vague and distant as the knights' differences.

For one thing, his position as Philosophy figure is blurred because in the analogies that exist between the *Consolation* and the tale, he doubles for Theodoric as well as Philosophy. He is the imprisoner as well as the liberator. Furthermore, his power is political rather than intellectual, as Philosophy's is, and such intellect as we see him exercise (especially in his final speech) is heavily tinged with what we feel to be only practical ulterior motives. In the confrontations of the tale, it is sometimes as if a Theodoric in disguise as Philosophy had come to Boethius to subvert his despair into an appreciation of Ostrogothic aims for empire. The ambivalence in Theseus's presentation at points leaves the impression of excessive mundanity and second-rate ideals, which causes us to move away from him in mild contempt.

For another thing, Theseus, unlike Philosophy, is shown in the context which includes the gods of the universe. They, not he, determine the issue of the tale, which knight shall have the lady, in answers to prayers of young men whom he has only laughed at. His lack of control over the center calls his power into question, and his ignorance of these divine happenings calls into question the quality of his knowledge. Until the gods mingle in human concerns, he reigns unchallenged before us, manipulating the destinies of all who encounter him. In the way appropriate to Menippean satire, and as with women and love, he gives the gods lip service. He mentions them in his speeches, builds temples to them. But just as he has no comprehension of the meaning of the world of beauty and love, so he has no comprehension that the gods form an order of existence completely alien to his own.

When the infernal fury kills his winner and voids his arrangement to satisfy a law independent of his authoritative contrivance, he is shocked by his failure and turns unconsolable to his father, Egeus, for an answer. All he is given is the inappropriate—for the context—tragical answer: Death is the fate of every man.

> "This world nys but a thurghfare ful of wo,
> And we been pilgrymes, passynge to and fro.
> Deeth is an ende of every worldly soore."
> (ll. 2847–49)

Thus Theseus, knowing nothing of the prayers or of the scenes in heaven, is left with this explanation far away from the actual state of affairs. Like his belief that his actions would solve the knights' problem, this answer becomes simply another of his glaring misapprehensions. To see Theseus in a universe where the gods take no note of him, where they, at least nominally, are the resolvers of the tale's major issue, quite independent of his initiative power, where the universe he imagines can be thought by no stretch of the imagination to coincide with the universe they preside in ("over" would suggest they have power which they too do not seem to have) is to diminish his significance, to throw him too into a backwash, away from that focus which would enable us to use his words to interpret the tale.

The diminishing of Theseus's stature in the public phase of the *disputatio* blunts the sharpness of the debate, but it is also blunted by Chaucer's giving him no direct opposite, no one to play Palamon to his Arcite. Hyppolyte, the obvious candidate, is silent. The other women at the center of the dialogue, the meeting in the grove, have no distinctive voice. They object to Theseus's killing the knights, not because they shun the all-too-ready, simplistic male solution "off with his head," but because the knights are men of such "high rank," a strictly patriarchal reason for abstaining. ("No rich man ever hanged" belongs to this syndrome of thought.) They are only secondarily concerned that the knights are in love and wounded. There is dramatic verisimilitude in that the out-group usually has to use the language of the in-group to succeed. But the point is that though Chaucer evokes the opposition of matriarchy and patriarchy, he fails to present the values of women and natural law in such a way as to give them objective status. In a general way, women present an opposing world view in the tale, but it is, as it were, without their knowledge, without the language which would objectify the importance of the opposition.

We view the entry of the gods into the *disputatio* with mixed feelings of relief and absurdity. On the one hand, they bring fresh air into the stalemate of the relations the knights have dwelt in with each other and with the world for so long; they turn the mockery of Theseus's tournament into something significant. On the other, in their farcical way, they solve the problems that mortals have been so unfortunate as to create without thought for human complexity. In the scene in heaven, the arbiters of the action present us with nothing so much as a willful child's temper tantrum being handled by the ingenuity of an evil nursemaid. Yet, perforce, their activities embody the divine aspects of the laws that operate in the human world. Saturn's solution represents happiness and immediate gratification of desire, which wins out over justice, a long-range investigation of the appropriate resolution of the knights' requests, which Jupiter shows no capacity for bringing to bear in the argument. The Golden Age triumphs over the Age of Iron, not because it has any divine values attached it it, but ultimately, it would seem, because of Palamon's more careful prayer. The Knight's absence of commentary, as with Palamon's success at the end of the tale, gives this victory no resonance.

The gods have the ordinary characteristics of *deus* figures in Menippean satire. That is to say that they are actual gods with Roman names, have a dramatic objectivity equivalent to the other characters, and are a part of a traditional mythological system to which the Knight pays no attention. Saturn, instead of uttering the words of a Golden Age god, berates the assembly with an account of the evil he presides over. Jupiter, instead of acting as the awesome controller of all things, is the harried, unsuccessful ruler trying to keep peace in the family. In addition, the gods are, according to the convention, concerned to give those with whom they deal what they ask for. Their first intrusion is in Mercury's appearance in Arcite's dream, proof perhaps that the answer to the *demande d'amour* is "Arcite," because his desire to see Emily again is intense enough to call up a god. Mercury's brief message to him, which, though redolent of that ambiguity for which Lucian attacks divine prophecies ("To Athenes shaltou wende, / Ther is thee shapen of thy wo an ende" [ll. 1391–92]), is also in accord with what he wants. In the temple the direct prayers of the knights are again heartfelt enough to create the awaited moment of fulfillment. The final appearance of a god, the fury that Pluto sends at Saturn's request, carries out the scheme, a warning perhaps, about the frightening ramifications of intense longing; for if Palamon desires Emily, he cannot have desired Arcite's death, much less the prolonged and painful suffering that precedes it.

Menippean satire's presentation of its *deus* figures functions as a method of breaking the power of mythic oppositions, of calling into question man's methods of telling the stories of the gods, one of his more elaborate methods of explanation. But in the Knight's Tale, Chaucer blurs even this impression, by placing the gods too in a context which moves the parodic concerns of the tale into a further dimension. The elation in the heaven where Saturn seems cleverly to find a way of resolving the dilemma posed by the gods' granting of what appear to be opposing requests stands as direct duplication of signs given in the temple. Palamon's sign shows a delay, but he knows that his boon is granted (ll. 2268–69). Arcite hears the dim, low word "Victory" (ll. 2431–33). In between, Emily, praying for whichever knight desires her most, receives this sign:

> For right anon oon of the fyres queynte,
> And quyked agayn, and after that anon
> That oother fyr was queynt and al agon.
>
> (ll. 2334–36)

These instant answers reflect exactly what happens later. The scene in heaven cannot be read as occurring simultaneously with the prayers because it is the word "victory" that sets off Venus's weeping.

The duplication—which indicates that these gods do not know what they are about—is a parodic representation of the relation between the Boethian concepts of fate and providence (bk. 4, pr. 6). Fate's function is to implement individual events, and the ability to control all these single manifestations in an orderly way is the function of providence. Mars and Venus have the first power; Saturn has the second. But in the *Consolation* the validity of the distinction between fate and providence depends on positing the existence of two states of being—time and eternity. In the Knight's Tale these gods live in time like Homer's gods, as is evident in the argument that rages *after* the prayers. Venus's vision is too confined for her to understand the scope of the pattern she is involved in; Saturn's, not quite providential enough to avoid thought. Because of their ignorance of what goes on at the shrines and because they have no freedom, no capacity to do other than follow out the decrees of destinal forces that operate above them in response to the desires of the young people praying, they, in what they do at least, seem to "function as metaphors of man's will" (Richard Neuse).

As the top of the paradigm of the two laws, this presentation of the gods undermines more drastically than any other of the Knight's "blurrings" the potential significance of the structure. With a more exalted conception of divinity before us, we could read the movement from private, to public, to divine portrayals of the conflict as the way to understanding. We would move from the knights' hopeless confusion, to the pragmatic blindness of Theseus, to the freedom of the celestial vision which understands the mutual reliance of one law on the other. Or if the peace created by Saturn had any of the depths and grandeur of the "Paradiso" or of the final book of the *Consolation,* we could read the poem as the narrator's account of the spiritual pilgrimage from beauty, to love, to happiness, the worlds which transcend force, legality, and categories. But these gods are far from providing confirmation of such a reading. The vision of Venus weeping at Saturn's knee over Mars's promise gives us either the impression that we view a more elementary stage of affairs than the society of earth must abide, or else an uneasy sensation that the universe is stranger than we think.

Instead of the movement upward, such as we get in Dante and Boethius, where the ideas move in ever-widening circles until at last we feel we are intellectually in the final rung of paradise, we encounter a deliberate parody of the thought that man can rise ever higher. The progression from beauty to love to happiness works only within the private phase of the debate and is represented in Emily. Beautiful in the garden, she inspires the knights' love for ten years. As the occasion for the tourney, she is a cause of peace and sublimation among men; the latent hatred between Thebes and Athens is quiet, the tournament being, of course, a much lesser conflict than war. But there is distracting evidence even at the human level. Emily relieves the knights' boredom and despair in prison, gives them hope, but the actions that love inspires are not such as to excite our admiration. In this period of confusion, the creativity the knights' love looses in them borders on madness: each projects, and Arcite actually lives, another version of actuality. Palamon projects a world in which Thebes is conqueror and Athens the defeated; Arcite becomes a servant, changes his class and name. The tourney Emily presides over in name is a further confusion to them and who they are: rulers of Thebes, enemies to Theseus.

It is in their period of confusion that we find their Boethian speeches, in which, sensing something of the horrors of the universe around them, they question the divine levels of the laws. Placed against the *Consolation,* the immediate effect of the speeches is to diminish the speakers. Boethius faces the loss of all material possessions, the desertion of his friends in the Senate, and the threat of physical death, but, worst of all, he wallows in a state of mind which threatens imminent spiritual death. The knights, like Boethius in prison, have also lost everything, but they are not threatened with either physical or spiritual death. They have indeed lost their friendship, friendship being in Philosophy's eyes of so high a spiritual value that it is beyond the control of Fortune (bk. 3, pr. 2), but they are too angry with one another to feel threatened by even this loss. Their deepest despair is in fact caused by a spiritual renewal, which they have found in their love for Emily. What frustrates them is that they cannot reach the experience they want, not the thought that they can never have it again. They are not saying, "The worst unhappiness is to have been happy," but rather, "The worst unhappiness is to contemplate an unattainable object of desire." The bittersweet despair of this experience is profoundly unlike the despair of total loss.

Seen as parts of a Menippean satire like the *Consolation*, the knights' speeches fare better. They deal with the underlying problem that man must solve when he becomes aware of the dualistic universe about him, when his familiar world turns out not to be the only world that exists. The *Consolation*, against which the speeches are implicitly set, is addressed to answer this problem. In his downfall Boethius becomes aware of a universe in which events in human life are haphazard, a universe in which good actions do not necessarily bring just rewards. The knights make a similar discovery of a chaotic universe that stands in opposition to the world of their former training, where everything was related by rules of kinship, oaths, and war. As Boethius's views are contradicted by Philosophy's arguing, so aspects of the Knight's Tale contradict the two speeches (Theseus, however, does not have this function). Palamon is a fatalist whose assumptions are proved wrong by events. Arcite, a man searching for God, is contradicted by the absence of any image that fulfills his hope.

Palamon's speech takes justice as its central theme, and this is in accord with his projective investigation of a world view not native to him, a world set up by the conventions of patriarchal society, a world which somehow bars him from Emily. The speech is parallel to book 1, meter 5, in the *Consolation,* Boethius's prayer to understand why man, who must view the evil triumphing and the good oppressed, is excluded from the goodness of the order than governs all else. But Palamon, unlike Boethius, does not put himself in the position of the innocent questioner. He laments with the belief that he already knows the answers which Boethius must go through the process of learning. The only point in which he admits himself ignorant is that state of affairs after death; otherwise, he thinks everything is fated. Men are no better than beasts; they suffer in innocence with the permission of the gods. Beasts have their will and die without dreams, but man must control himself and suffer torment after death in spite of the torment he had in life. Serpents and thieves who have injured men go free, while the gods oppress him and his city. His bitterness springs from a despair, opened to him by love, about the unpleasantness of the alternate world. The most rigid of the projected conclusions about divine governance of men's affairs, Palamon's thoughts are almost as fatalistic as Troilus's.

But in spite of its desperate seriousness, his speech is in many respects a kind of empty exercise reflecting his frustrated but complacent assurance that his views are the correct ones (e.g., his rigid refusal to enter into discussion with Arcite over the new problems posed by Emily). A belief in fate is a great protector of his biased conviction. His statement that animals have a better life than men is not susceptible of proof or contradiction, and is a maxim always comforting when men try to prove their right to despair. But his statement that the guilty go free and the innocent suffer is not borne out well by the tale. In his own view of things, he deserved Emily because he saw her first; in the end he has possession. This connection is sometimes felt as a poorly realized example of poetic justice in the tale; nevertheless, it refutes Palamon's assumption in the complaint, and is a change that Chaucer makes in the *Teseida,* where Arcite sees Emily first. Palamon's speech climaxes in his description of the gods who imprison him and destroy Thebes. But he succeeds in freeing himself, and while Theseus has destroyed the city, it has not been razed, for Palamon and Arcite set off again "To Thebes, with his olde walles wyde" (l. 1880). He laments, then, not from a feeling of alienation and abandonment in a universe without order, as Boethius does, but from anger at the cruel auspices under which man—in particular, Palamon—is compelled to exist. There is no sense of a helpless involvement in a universal dilemma or, subsequently, of the magnificent power of the human mind to transcend what might appear to be the cruelty of the gods. These two conceptions, of course, distinguish the *Consolation* from the momentarily irritated thoughts of a young man.

Arcite's complaint takes happiness as its central theme, a concern also out of accord with his temperament. The measure of his dislocation is revealed by his tendency at this moment to identify with the world of Emily and all she represents, a world in which happiness is as central a concern as love, beauty, and peace. His extreme unhappiness springs from his inability to understand how to penetrate this world. His lament, as that of a questioner who must work out an answer, is more serious than Palamon's. His subject, happiness, is taken, not from book 1 of the *Consolation,* but from book 3, from words spoken by Philosophy rather than by Boethius. But while Philosophy comfortably elaborates on the subject, Arcite can only ask despairing questions. In Philosophy's discussion, happiness is the initial stage in her argument that all men naturally desire God. Arcite, on the contrary, can only lament at the state of affairs. He is torn by the ironic confusion of means and ends, efforts and attainments. The gods give man something good, and he does not realize it until he has lost it; men ask for something and receive it in a way that they had not contemplated. For all his struggle, Arcite cannot rise to the level of transcendence required of the Philosophy figure or see the majestic implications of his own visions. Surrounding Arcite's Boethianism is mundanity which makes his despair seem trivial in comparison with the discussion in the *Consolation.*

As the comparison with the corresponding passages in the *Consolation* implies, Arcite's speech is based on the need to strive for God. But there is nothing in the tale that embodies this "god." Beauty, love, happiness, and peace seem to us all uncontrovertible ideals, and our underlying tendency, therefore, is to sympathize with Arcite. But the tale offers no evidence that anyone possesses this world—certainly not the women, either Hyppolyte or the women at the grove, to whom its possession has been traditionally ascribed and is so ascribed by the male characters in the tale. Emily, the chief inspirer of visions in the knights, knows nothing of it, and possesses neither power nor inclination to take the knights back to Scythia, as it were. Her prayer to Diana, her one positive act in the tale, betrays only the faintest interest in Theseus's world, where marriage has a status equal to war as a controlling device. But there is no rebellion or antagonism at being used as a pawn. Her pale indifference toward the knights reminds us of the attitude of Tennyson's gods, who listen to man's pleas as a "tale of little meaning though the words are strong." And while, on the one hand, her attitude here will serve to remind us of the strange nature of divinity so often depicted in the tale, it will not, on the other, make us think she could have given Arcite what he sought. It may be argued that he knew that, and chose to worship her at a distance, and did not approach her for the physical purposes of marriage when he returned to Athens in disguise. The scene with the gods—which, in its own callous way, embodies the abstract conflict—offers no resting place for the values toward which Arcite moves. The context of the tale makes Arcite's search an unrealizable dream.

Because of the miscalculation in his prayer, he is the object of the plot's most obvious irony, his life being the example of the truth of his own momentary understanding: "We witen nat what thing we preyen heere" (1. 1260). He is the object of its poetic justice. The answer to his question, "Who may give a lover any law?" is answered in the outcome. It is he who initiates the death of friendship, and it is he who is punished. Although the tale as a whole does not allow Arcite the rank of tragic hero, for the Knight's vision contains too many possibilities, he has his attributes. His failure to find his new world is acknowledged in his death speech; he dies affirming the values of the brotherhood he has rejected and crying out in the arms of Emily for mercy. We may interpret his pleas as the desire for the impossible synthesis of the best of both worlds, devoid of error and ultimate destruction. This synthesis is what a different portrayal of the gods might have given us; instead the Knight presents it only as a dying man's hopeless dream.

The echoes of Boethius in the knights' speeches help to hold in ironic counterpoise the events and descriptions in the tale which relate to them. In this light they are parodies of human attempts at understanding the universe. The speeches, like those in the *Consolation,* represent the tableaux of thought, the Chaucerian speeches less well objectified than Boethius's. In the overall scheme of things, the speeches are fragments which attempt to project a pattern of coherence. In themselves, the uttering of such words helps man for a moment to create the illusion that somewhere or other there is wholeness and clarity. In the face of a chaotic universe, the knights' visions embody aids to the belief in the presence of an ideal system. Behind the tableaux lurk the informalizable, the contradictory, the unimaginable. The narrator's failure to reconcile the dichotomies implied by the presence of a "this world and the other" or even to comment on them sets up a sense of constant contradiction, not to say abandonment. The omission of such explanation and the apparent indifference to the blatant and subtle incongruities that ultimately arise from the continual presentation of unresolved views leaves an uninterpretable universe reduced to intelligibility only momentarily by those who try to describe it.

The mythic worlds, evoked, transmuted by the power of the present to alter any myth, then discarded as if irrelevant to the conflicts they survive from, loom and disappear in the Knight's Tale. The texture of the universe portrayed remains vague, uncertain. The ancient oppositions are continually thrusting themselves to the fore: Titans and Olympians, Golden Age/Age of Iron, matriarchy/patriarchy, natural law/human law, Boethius's vision/Philosophy's vision. The first members of each set form a syndrome of overlapping agreements, and so do the second. Historically speaking, the last member of each pair is thought to have superseded the first. But of course, Menippean satire would not for good reason propose that the human race ever suppressed any one of its ideas by any means so simple as the passage of time, much less by a war which ended in a victory both sides agreed to. Nor does the Knight's Tale. The oppositions which figure in its structure are continually present for our enrichment and also, inevitably, for our confusion. The Titan Saturn and the Olympian Jupiter coexist in the heavens, intent on a conflict which has nothing whatsoever to do with the war that destroyed the Golden Age and instituted the Age of Iron. An Amazon can marry a Theban, neither having manifested any interest in the opposing values they mythically represent. The laws of love and loyalty set up conflicts which are never resolved. The Boethian knights and their struggles stay in our minds quite as clearly as Philosophy-Theseus's superficial, accidental success.

The effect of the Knight's portrayal of the gods, the diminishing of the Philosophy figure Theseus, his indifference toward the ideals of the knights, his parodic treatment of their efforts to attain the vision of the *Consolation,* is to make the conflict of the laws appear man-created, in medieval terms nominalistic rather than idealistic, arbitrary categories which contain neither any certifiable truth nor the capacity to hold up under continuous application to a universe that will not let itself be controlled by any human idea. This is commonplace thought for Menippean satire, but again we encounter that extra level of perception in the tale, the feeling that while there is a definite need to draw on the oppositions of natural and positive law because there seem to be no others for this story, neither the opposition nor one of the views warrants the energy of desperate commitment. The failure seems not to matter very much.

Chaucer's techniques in the tale, which evoke but then ignore these primal conflicts and categories, have not met with universal approval. Baldwin, for instance, writes: "That Chaucer's voice could falter and be unsure of itself is apparent in the Knight's Tale, technically, perhaps, one of the poorest of his works. There the severe abridgement of his source, Boccaccio's *Teseida*, especially with the device of *occupatio*; the incompatibility of such motifs as classical Fortune and romantic chance; and the tendency for the narrative to shift focus awkwardly—these seem to indicate a clumsy voice and an early Chaucer as well." Salter also feels that Chaucer has failed to control the material in the tale. I am myself convinced that the tale is the most heavily revised of all Chaucer's works. There is an extraordinary sense of total control, total lack of spontaneity about it, and consequently an overwhelming feeling of déjà vu. But I believe that Chaucer stopped revising because he had succeeded in creating the effect he sought and that this effect was the portrayal of a certain kind of narrator, whose observation adds that level of irony which makes this Menippean satire distinctive.

An Opening: The Knight's Tale

Helen Cooper

The Knight's Tale is a dynamic introduction to the storytelling: it leads in many directions and opens out on to many of the problems and perspectives explored later in the work. Many of the reflections of it that occur later are very precise indeed, as in the parodies given by the Miller's and Merchant's Tales; I shall discuss connections of this kind, of specific echoes of plot motif or rhetorical commonplaces [elsewhere], for they only affect the Knight's Tale by hindsight. My concern here is with the tale alone, as it stands—for there is as yet at this point in the work nothing apart from the General Prologue to relate it to. What emerges most clearly from the Knight's Tale by itself is the immensity of the issues it raises. These themes are not complete in themselves, as plot motifs are, but are often presented as questions. Later stories take up the questions in different forms, or occasionally even suggest answers; but all such concerns open out from the first of the tales. This open-ended exploration is contained in a brilliantly controlled narrative and rhetorical structure, and given form through a handling of genre that in itself suggests that there is no single or simple way of looking at the world. The tales in which Chaucer brings together different genres are indeed often the finest in the whole work, and the Knight's Tale acts as the model.

The Host had requested stories "of aventures that whilom

From *The Structure of the* Canterbury Tales. © 1983 by Helen Cooper. Gerald Duckworth, 1983.

han bifalle"; "once upon a time" stories. The Knight takes up the injunction very precisely, but at once endows it with a force and breadth such as the original formula had not suggested:

> Whilom, as olde stories tellen us,
> Ther was a duc that highte Theseus;
> Of Atthenes he was lord and governour,
> And in his tyme swich a conquerour,
> That gretter was ther noon under the sonne.
> Ful many a riche contree hadde he wonne.
>
> (ll. 859–64, F. N. Robinson, 2d ed.)

The lines immediately establish a sense of epic range and grandeur. This impression is reinforced by the epigraph from Statius's *Thebaid* that heads the tale in some manuscripts, lines which not only introduce the action of the tale but affirm its antecedents in heroic poetry. ("Iamque domos patrias, Scithice post aspera gentis / Proelia, laurigero, &c. [And now after his fierce battles with the Scythians, (Theseus approached) his native land in his laurel-decked (chariot)]" [*Thebaid,* bk. 12, ll. 519–20]. The epigraph may have been added by copyists, but the point remains the same whether it was Chaucer or a scribe who saw the epic appropriateness of the lines.) This aspect of the tale has sometimes been played down, since Chaucer reduces the epic qualities of his major source, Boccaccio's *Teseida* (a "Theseid" to match the "Aeneid"); but Dryden, who did not have the *Teseida* to contrast it with, still saw the work as an epic. For him it was "the Noble Poem of Palamon and Arcite, which is of the Epique kind, and perhaps not much inferiour to the *Ilias* or the *Aeneis.*"

Chaucer does none the less concentrate on the romance elements in the story. His poem is only a fifth the length of Boccaccio's, and it is the heroic sections of legendary history and military campaigns that are most ruthlessly cut. Love, and the lovers' rivalry, come to dominate the tale; but the epic quality of the poem has still been affirmed strongly in the opening section. Chaucer differentiates the five romances of the *Canterbury Tales* very precisely. The Wife of Bath's Tale comes from the edge of the genre where romance touches folk tale; the Squire's Tale is the opening of an interlaced romance; the Franklin's is a Breton lai; *Sir Thopas* is a parody of the popular romance. The Knight's Tale starts the sequence at the noblest level, where romance shares a border with epic.

Romance and epic are on a single narrative continuum; but Chaucer rapidly qualifies the nature of the Knight's Tale as a romance in a more startling way, by fusing it with its opposite, tragedy—tragedy in that Boethian sense of the "unwar strookes" of Fortune. Romance has more than a conventional expectation of a happy ending: generically it is partially definable in terms of the upward movement of Fortune's wheel. At the very beginning of the story, before the introduction of Palamon and Arcite and the main action, Chaucer insists on this contrast, that one man's victory is another's overthrow. As Theseus enters Athens in triumph he is met by "a compaignye of ladyes," dressed in black, who kneel before him to ask for his help. The oldest of them, widow of King Capaneus, addresses him like this:

> "Lord, to whom Fortune hath yiven
> Victorie, and as a conqueror to lyven
>
> .   .   .   .
>
> Certes, lord, ther is noon of us alle,
> That she ne hath been a duchesse or a queene.
> Now be we caytyves, as it is wel seene,
> Thanked be Fortune and hire false wheel,
> That noon estaat assureth to be weel."
>
> (ll. 915–16, 922–26)

Capaneus himself is a victim of Fortune in the manner of the subjects of the Monk's tragedies. This is the first of many passages emphasising the mingled web of good and ill, joy and grief, in the world. The romance vision is one of suffering and hardship as a means to a blissful ending; the vision of the Knight's Tale is more complex. The ladies beg Theseus to attack Creon, lord of Thebes, who has not only killed their husbands but refused them burial and "maketh houndes ete hem in despite." Theseus responds to their plea for "som drope of pitee"; and he at once sets off to attack Creon "as he that hadde his deeth ful wel deserved," to act as the agent of justice and restore the decencies of human order. But to get to the ceremony of the funeral pyre, Theseus must first destroy the city; and his victory brings with it not only the restoration of the proper ceremonial obsequies and a new triumphal entry, but, for Palamon and Arcite, discovered among the heaps of the dead, perpetual imprisonment. The contrast is again brought out by sharp juxtaposition:

> Hoom he rit anon
> With laurer crowned as a conquerour;
> And ther he lyveth in joye and in honour
> Terme of his lyf; what nedeth wordes mo?
> And in a tour, in angwissh and in wo,
> This Palamon and his felaw Arcite
> For everemoore.
>
> (ll. 1026–32)

Only at the very end of the Knight's Tale—and perhaps not even there—are we allowed to think of joy without also thinking of its opposite. The poem is Palamon's romance, in which his faithfulness and endurance at last win him his lady; but it is at the same time the tragedy of Arcite, whose equal mental suffering and greater physical pain are rewarded only by death.

The architectonic form in which these generic contrasts are held is one of Chaucer's most remarkable, and unsung, achievements. He compressed Boccaccio's lengthy amplification of the story into a much tighter structure of a kind only paralleled in contemporary literature by *Sir Gawain and the Green Knight*—to which indeed it bears a surprisingly close resemblance. Both works are structured symmetrically, with equivalent scenes or episodes occurring at each end and working inwards toward a crucial central core of three: the three bedroom scenes and hunts in *Gawain,* the three temples in the Knight's Tale. The triads are central in both senses: they occupy the midpoint of this symmetrical structure (though they occur in the third of each poem's four sections); and they are also in some way definitive for the rest of the work.

Such symmetry of structure is very unusual indeed in the Middle Ages. (I mean specifically symmetry of the kind that works from the outside in. Repeated patterns are often found in romances.) Most mediaeval imaginative literature operates on a linear basis, often represented in the narrative by a journey. All romance quests do this; so does the *Divine Comedy,* with Dante's journey from Hell to Heaven; so do many saints' lives, such as the voyages of St. Brendan; so does *Piers Plowman,* though the dreamer's journeying is located only in the field full of folk; so does the *Canterbury Tales* itself, with its pilgrimage frame. That the hero returns to his society at the end of his quest, or that Chaucer may have intended to bring his pilgrims back to the Tabard, does not significantly affect this linearity. In *Gawain,* however, there is a careful mirroring of events and even lines: the references to Troy at the beginning and end; within those, the scenes at Camelot; the references to Arthur as Gawain's uncle and to Morgan as his aunt; the beheading and the return blow; the winter journeys to Bertilak's castle and the Green Chapel. The Knight's Tale works similarly. It opens and closes with a wedding: Theseus's to Hippolyta at the beginning, Palamon's to Emily at the end. Within those are the two funeral scenes, of the pyres for the widows' husbands at the start, for Arcite at the end. After the first of these comes the lovers' rivalry for Emily; before the last, Arcite yields her to Palamon. Arcite's metaphorical death at his exile from Emily, which results in an illness so severe that he is no longer recognisable for his old self and so can return under a new identity, is balanced by his actual death. (This is the one point where the strict symmetry of the mirror effect is broken, in that according to that arrangement his death should precede his entrusting of Emily to Palamon—an obvious narrative impossibility. The overall effect of the sequence is not disturbed. A similar thing happens in *Gawain,* where the episodes of his arming necessarily come before the two journeys.) The fight in the wood gives way in the second half of the poem to the tournament. At the centre is the triad of the three temples, of Venus, Mars and Diana, described with iconographic detail that gives them a significance extending far beyond the confines of the poem.

The symmetrical structuring of the Knight's Tale accounts for less of the poem than it does for *Sir Gawain,* but in Chaucer's work it runs alongside other structural patterns. The initial episode, of the widows' appeal for help and the destruction of Thebes, acts rather like the prologues to the dream poems, to introduce and reflect on some of the main themes by juxtaposition. It serves to define the poem as something more than romance: grief, death, and the imposition of order on disorder are its dominant motifs. It is also the first of several repeated sequences in the tale. The opening series of the widows kneeling to ask for mercy, the battle at Thebes and the funeral is repeated on a larger scale later, when the ladies fall on their knees to beg mercy for the lovers, the tournament takes place and Arcite's body is burnt. The parallelism of phrasing is at times very striking:

> Ther kneled in the heighe weye
> A compaignye of ladyes
>
> (ll. 897–98)

who cry,

> "Have on us wrecched wommen som mercy!"
>
> (l. 950)

In the forest, "all the ladyes in the campaignye" cry

> "Have mercy, Lord, upon us wommen alle!"
> And on hir bare knees adoun they falle.
>
> (ll. 1757–58)

On both occasions the "gentil duc" reacts "with herte pitous" (ll. 952–53),

> For pitee renneth soone in gentil herte.
>
> (l. 1761)

The funeral obsequies are not the only ceremony to be repeated: Emily's "observaunce" of May when the cousins see her in the garden is repeated in Arcite's maying in the forest, and both episodes lead to rivalry between the knights, the first time a quarrel, the second a combat. In both cases the darkness of disorder replaces the brilliance of the celebrations of "faire, fresshe May."

There are a number of other striking oppositions of this kind. Before the cousins' quarrel, Emily's appearance in the garden, with all the densely clustered imagery of colour, lilies and roses, the daybreak and the spring, is brought up sharply against the fact of the knights' imprisonment: garden and prison are literally as well as thematically contiguous. The passage is worth quoting at length as it shows so well Chaucer's superb manipulation of conventional materials: by their means he defines Emily as the ideal romance heroine par excellence, unsurpassable in beauty and symbolic association, and so the inevitable object of the cousins' adoration.

> It fil ones, in a morwe of May,
> That Emelye, that fairer was to sene
> Than is the lylie upon his stalke grene,
> And fressher than the May with floures newe—
> For with the rose colour stroof hire hewe,
> I noot which was the fyner of hem two—

Er it were day, as was hir wone to do,
She was arisen and al redy dight

.　.　.　.　.　.　.　.　.　.

Yclothed was she fressh, for to devyse:
Hir yelow heer was broyded in a tresse
Bihynde hir bak, a yerde long, I gesse.
And in the gardyn, at the sonne upriste,
She walketh up and doun, and as hire liste
She gadereth floures, party white and rede,
To make a subtil gerland for hire hede;
And as an aungel hevenysshly she soong.
The grete tour, that was so thikke and stroong,
Which of the castel was the chief dongeoun,
(Ther as the knyghtes weren in prisoun
Of which I tolde yow and tellen shal)
Was evene joynant to the gardyn wal
There as this Emelye hadde hir pleyynge.
Bright was the sonne and cleer that morwenynge,
And Palamoun, this woful prisoner,
As was his wone, by leve of his gayler,
Was risen and romed in a chambre an heigh.

(ll. 1034–41, 1048–65)

As in the opening scene of Theseus's triumph and the weeping
widows, the light and dark sides of life are inextricable.

Chaucer also uses juxtaposition to contrast ideal action with its
opposite. The cousins have a violent quarrel over who has the first
claim on Emily, and Arcite brutally renounces the values of blood
relationship and of sworn brotherhood in favour of love:

" 'Who shall yeve a lovere any lawe?'

.　.　.　.　.　.　.　.　.　.

And therfore, at the kynges court, my brother,
Ech man for hymself, ther is noon oother."

(ll. 1164, 1181–82)

This is immediately followed by a reference to the love between
Perotheus and Theseus, which was so great

That whan that oon was deed, soothly to telle,
His felawe wente and soughte hym doun in helle.

(ll. 1199–1200)

The Classical legend of Pirithous is different: it is Chaucer who specifically turns it into an example of friendship stronger than death. The same contrast of ideal brotherhood with actual enmity is expressed more concisely, almost with the force of oxymoron, in the preparations for the fight in the forest—a fight intended to be to the death:

> Ther nas no good day, ne no saluyng,
> But streight, withouten word or rehersyng,
> Everich of hem heelp for to armen oother
> As freendly as he were his owene brother.
>
> (ll. 1649–52)

The irony lies in the fact that they are indeed "brothers" by oath and kinship.

These structural and thematic oppositions reach a climax in the descriptions of the three temples. It is there, at the centre of the mirror patterning of the work, that the strongest statement of the disorder of the world is made. The lovers had complained against the state of the universe, and their complaints were more than the expression of mere personal opinion; but they were nonetheless in the first instance dramatic utterances appropriate to the speaker and his circumstances. The descriptions of the gods are presented as incontrovertible fact. These gods are not mythic fictions: as planetary influences they represent the literal truth of life in the world.

They shock in the first instance because they are not what one expects. In a courtly romance the principles of decorum would seem to prescribe idealised gods, an enchantingly beautiful Venus, a Mars in glittering armour, a Belphoebe-like Diana. Chaucer has established from the beginning, however, that such a mode of easy idealism is alien to this work, and he presents the gods as emblematic of all the cosmic capriciousness and disorder the human characters have sensed. Good and bad now appear not merely juxtaposed but inextricably jumbled. Lovers' oaths, hope, rashness, beauty, pimping, riches, rape and jealousy are tumbled out in a single heap as morally indistinguishable attributes of Venus: "wroght on the wal" of her temple are

> The firy strokes of the desirynge
> That loves servantz in this lyf enduren;
> The othes that hir covenantz assuren;
> Plesaunce and Hope, Desir, Foolhardynesse,
> Beautee and Youthe, Bauderie, Richesse,

> Charmes and Force, Lesynges, Flaterye,
> Despense, Bisynesse, and Jalousye,
> That wered of yelewe gooldes a gerland,
> And a cokkow sittynge on hir hand.
>
> (ll. 1922–30)

The *exempla* that follow, of famous lovers of legend, are equally suspect. Some died for love; passion led Solomon to "folye"; the enchantments of Medea and Circe are ascribed to Venus. Arcite had denied that any law could be stronger than love, and the account of Venus's temple leads to a conclusion that gives his denial the force of divinely sanctioned truth.

> Thus may ye seen that wysdom ne richesse,
> Beautee ne sleighte, strengthe ne hardynesse,
> Ne May with Venus holde champartie,
> For as hir list the world than may she gye.
>
> (ll. 1947–50)

This is a vision of the world very different from the "faire cheyne of love" binding the cosmos that Theseus envisages. Venus overturns all human ideals of moral action.

The temple of Mars is even nastier. He is the god not only of battle—that is mentioned surprisingly little—but of all irrational violence: of theft and conspiracy, suicide and murder, human and animal blood-lust, fatal accidents:

> Ther saugh I first the derke ymaginyng
> Of Felonye, and al the compassyng;
> The crueel Ire, reed as any gleede;
> The pykepurs, and eek the pale Drede;
> The smylere with the knyf under the cloke;
> The shepne brennynge with the blake smoke;
> The tresoun of the mordrynge in the bedde;
> The open werre, with woundes al bibledde;
> Contek, with blody knyf and sharp manace.
>
> (ll. 1995–2003)

> Amyddes of the temple sat Meschaunce.
>
> (l. 2009)

> The careyne in the busk, with throte ycorve;
> A thousand slayn, and nat of qualm ystorve;

> The tiraunt, with the pray by force yraft;
> The toun destroyed, ther was no thyng laft.
> Yet saugh I brent the shippes hoppesteres;
> The hunte strangled with the wilde beres;
> The sowe freeten the child right in the cradel;
> The cook yscalded, for al his longe ladel.
> Noght was foryeten by the infortune of Marte
> The cartere overryden with his carte:
> Under the wheel ful lowe he lay adoun.
>
> (ll. 2012–23)

That final image gives a startlingly literal interpretation to an image associated with the wheel of Fortune. It is not only the great who fall (though they are there too, in the next section, with Conquest "sittynge in greet honour" with a sword suspended above him by a thread); there is no condition of life that is safe from the power of these gods. Carters and tyrants are alike crushed. It is no surprise when Arcite, who commits himself to this god of casualities, dies a victim of "meschaunce."

Diana would seem to offer the fewest opportunities for such a bleak interpretation, but she provides no alleviation of this pessimistic vision. Her role as goddess of chastity is mentioned briefly at the start, but Chaucer swiftly moves on to less attractive aspects of her influence. As the lunar deity, she is the principle of change:

> Undernethe hir feet she hadde a moone,—
> Wexynge it was and sholde wanye soone.
>
> (ll. 2077–78)

Such a theme is appropriate for the narrative since Emily must change her allegiance from maidenhood to marriage; but if that is a positive transformation, the "change" depicted in the temple is not. The very ordering of waxing followed by waning implies a falling away, the downward turn of Fortune's wheel. The specific examples of transformation are of a more sinister violence. Chaucer's avoidance throughout the rest of his work of the metamorphosis of man into a lower order of life has already been mentioned; this passage is the great exception.

> Ther saugh I how woful Calistopee,
> Whan that Diane agreved was with here,
> Was turned from a womman til a bere.
>
> (ll. 2056–58)

> Ther saugh I Dane, yturned til a tree.
>
> (l. 2062)

> Ther saugh I Attheon an hert ymaked,
> For vengeaunce that he saugh Diane al naked;
> I saugh how that his houndes have hym caught
> And freten hym, for that they knewe hym naught.
>
> (ll. 2065–68)

The violence and the reduction of human being to passive victim are of a piece with the descriptions of the activities of Mars and Venus. As triple Hecate, Diana also has connections with the "derke regioun" of Pluto. Her role as Lucina, goddess of childbirth, is depicted as non-ideally as all the rest: the woman in labour who cries out to her for help "for hir child so longe was unborn" is given no assurance of survival.

The other gods who play some part in the tale are similarly presented. Juno is invariably mentioned with horror by the Theban princes. Arcite dreams that Mercury appears to him and bids,

> "To Atthenes shaltou wende,
> Ther is thee shapen of thy wo an ende."
>
> (ll. 1391–92)

He follows the advice; but the god's implied promise of hope is cruelly misleading, for the "ende" prepared for his woe is not joy but death. Saturn is the most sinister of them all:

> Myn is the drenchyng in the see so wan;
> Myn is the prison in the derke cote;
> Myn is the stranglyng and hangyng by the throte.
>
> (ll. 2456–58)

In the careful parallelism between the human and divine characters, Emily is paired with Diana, Palamon with Venus, Arcite with Mars. Since Saturn resolves the dispute between the other gods, it might be expected that Theseus would correspond to him; but Chaucer does not allow this to happen. Theseus's father Egeus indeed seems to be introduced partly to forestall such an equation. Theseus is associated with the other three gods—he bears Mars on his banner, he has been a "servant" of love in his youth, and in going hunting, "after Mars he serveth now Dyane." In his closing speech on the metaphysical ordering of the universe he looks beyond these three, and beyond anything Saturn can represent, to a philosophical or divine principle, the "First Moevere," whom he identifies with Jupiter. Jupiter has already made a brief appearance (l. 2442) as a rather ineffective peacemaker in the quarrel between the gods; the contrast between his inadequacy at that point and the omnipotent role Theseus ascribes to him highlights the difference between pagan pantheon and Christian truth. Theseus has no other name to give his First Mover. His identification is wrong, but his understanding of a higher divine providential principle beyond the capriciousness and cruelty of the lesser forces of destiny is certainly more important than his limited interpretation. For over two thousand lines of the narrative, the supernatural order is seen as a principle of disorder, disrupting all human attempts to live by ideals. Only in the last two hundred lines is there any indication that those ideals may have a "parfit and stable" root beyond the mutability of the world.

It is an answer, of sorts; but it does not altogether resolve the problem. Arcite has died still questioning the nature of "felicity" with ever greater urgency:

> What is this world? what asketh men to have?
> Now with his love, now in his colde grave
> Allone, withouten any compaignye.
>
> (l. 2777–79)

Theseus's final great speech gives an answer in terms of faith, and offers a pragmatic solution that enables life to continue; but the question remains central to human thought and experience.

Not even this much of an answer is given until the very end. In the body of the poem the characters feel themselves helpless before the forces of destiny or the gods. At its simplest, this helplessness means that when they are at the bottom of the wheel they know they must endure patiently. The widows deny that they are grieved by Theseus's "glorie and honour"; Arcite urges patience on Palamon when he cries out in prison. Such reactions at least imply a kind of understanding, that the universe is predictable though unpleasant; but things are rarely so straightforward. The cousins' inability to measure their own state is more unsettling. The damned and the saved in Dante's great *summa* at least know where they are; not so Arcite, released from prison at Perotheus's intercession, only to be exiled out of sight of Emily.

> He sayde, "Allas that day that I was born!
> Now is my prisoun worse than biforn;
> Now is me shape eternally to dwelle
> Noght in purgatorie, but in helle.
> Allas, that evere knew I Perotheus!
> For elles hadde I dwelled with Theseus,
> Yfetered in his prisoun everemo.
> Thanne hadde I been in blisse, and nat in wo."
>
> (ll. 1223–30)

Only the proof will distinguish hell from heaven—and perhaps not even that, for at this point each of the cousins bitterly envies the other. There is no way of knowing how to achieve one's desire. Providence and Fortune may appear in such strange forms as to be unrecognisable. Arcite continues with a lament broadened out from a consideration of his own state to the state of mankind:

> Allas, why pleynen folk so in commune
> Or purveiaunce of God, or of Fortune,
> That yeveth hem ful ofte in many a gyse
> Wel bettre than they kan hemself devyse?
>
> (ll. 1251–54)

A man may be murdered when he achieves the riches or the release from prison that he has desired:

> We witen nat what thing we prayen heere:
> We faren as he that dronke is as a mous.
> A dronke man woot wel he hath an hous,
> But he noot which the righte wey is thider,
> And to a dronke man the wey is slider.
> And certes, in this world so faren we;
> We seken fast after felicitee,
> But we goon wrong ful often, trewely.
>
> (ll. 1260–67)

Universal in implication as the lines are, they are also especially appropriate to Arcite, who throughout the story confuses ends and means. He

> wende and hadde a greet opinioun
> That if I myghte escapen from prisoun,

> Thanne hadde I been in joye and perfit heele,
> Ther now I am exiled fro my wele.
>
> (ll. 1269–72)

Later, before the tournament, he prays for victory, only to find that his triumph is hollow. His speeches on the state of the world are thus a dramatic projection; but they work the other way too— Chaucer wants this point of view to be expressed, and he puts Arcite into the appropriate situations to express it.

Palamon knows what he wants—Emily—and never loses sight of that; but his suffering is just as intense, and just as all-embracing in its implications. Chaucer always stresses the parallelism of the two knights, from the moment when they are found lying side by side on the battlefield wearing identical coats of arms. Each has a great speech in which he declares his love for Emily, and each denounces the condition of human life. Where Arcite laments man's erring pursuit of felicity, Palamon indicts the "cruel goddes" and their capricious, even vicious, control of human affairs. He too sees man as little better than a beast:

> What is mankynde moore unto you holde
> Than is the sheep that rouketh in the folde?
> For slayn is man right as another beest.
>
> (ll. 1307–9)

A beast, moreover, ends its suffering with death, whereas

> man after his deeth moot wepe and pleyne,
> Though in this world he have care and wo.
>
> (ll. 1320–21)

It is Palamon who asks the question that echoes down through the *Canterbury Tales,* and indeed through the whole history of metaphysical thought:

> What governance is in this prescience,
> That giltelees tormenteth innocence?
>
> (ll. 1313–14)

Different answers are given in different tales according to the system of values they adopt; for the moment Palamon does not attempt to answer it.

> The answere of this lete I to dyvynys,
>
> (l. 1323)

but the theological answers have never been entirely satisfactory.

The gods who take the greatest part in the action of the Knight's Tale, Saturn, Mars, Venus and Diana, are all seen as malevolent. As planetary deities they are agents of destiny or Fortune:

> Fortune hath yeven us this adversitee.
> Som wikke aspect or disposicioun
> Of Saturne, by som constellacioun,
> Hath yeven us this.
>
> (ll. 1086–89)

Theseus's attempts to impose order on the chaos of fortune are more persistent than successful. His retribution on Creon leads to the downfall of Thebes; his replacing of the fight in the forest by a tournament ends in death for the victor. He is nonetheless an ideal figure, a man of "pitee," "gentilesse," justice and mercy; but he is acting in an imperfect universe. The speeches on the state of the world that Chaucer gives to the knights are drawn from Boethius, from the prisoner's bitter attacks on Providence. Theseus's great closing speech is again Boethian, but taken this time from Philosophia's answers to Boethius's complaints.

> The Firste Moevere of the cause above,
> Whan he first made the faire cheyne of love,
> Greet was th'effect, and heigh was his entente.
>
> (ll. 2987–89)

There is a strong implication, however, that this is a matter to be taken on trust: the events of the tale hardly justify it, least of all the presentation of the gods. Theseus is making a declaration of faith; a faith that also has implications for action.

> Thanne is it wysdom, as it thynketh me,
> To maken vertue of necessitee,
> And take it weel that we may nat eschue.
>
> (ll. 3041–43)

This may sound like a doctrine of passive acceptance, but it is more than that. It is true that in contrast to almost every other romance the Knight's Tale stresses endurance rather than action, but Theseus's own interpretation of his dictum is more positive. He will stress the making virtue more than the necessity; and he accordingly marries Palamon to Emily to produce a happy ending from the tragedy like a conjuror's rabbit. "Making virtue of necessity" thus becomes closer to the conventional generic perspective of the romance than one might expect: it turns into something very similar to the idea of taking the adventure that shall fall to you, accepting the challenge of the quest, in a way that turns passive endurance into active heroic endeavour. Old Egeus insists on a more tragic view of life. He is given a speech stressing the universality of death, which is platitudinous only because it is self-evidently and incontrovertibly true; and he uses the familiar metaphor of life as a pilgrimage. Theseus redefines the idea of the "thurghfare ful of wo" into something more like a quest, and even produces the reward at the end of it in the shape of Emily. In the marriage, the human story and its metaphysical implications come together. The "faire cheyne of love" binds the cosmos and the elements; it is also the force that brings together nations into alliance and people to matrimony. That Palamon finally achieves Emily is a way of transcending the capriciousness of fortune to enact one's faith in the stability of the First Mover.

It is a process that comes impressively close to the heart of romance. As Northrop Frye has expounded, romance is the mode of the natural cycle through winter to spring, through death to rebirth—the same turning that Chaucer envisages as the fall and rise of Fortune's wheel, but projected on to a series of more mythic metaphors and truths. It is also the essence of Christian doctrine, where death is superseded by resurrection. Christianity is the religion of romance. The Knight's Tale is not a Christian allegory; it is, consciously, a Christian analogy, in which the affirmation of continuing life after Arcite's death is seen as a reflection of the ultimate providential ordering of the universe. The setting is pagan: Palamon and Arcite have none of the special insight into God's workings vouchsafed to the saint. All they can see are the operations of Fortune and the malevolent gods, and those are very disordered indeed. But there is a higher vision possible, and it is there that Chaucer ends.

The depth of meaning in the Knight's Tale is impressive. Courtly romances since the time of Chretien de Troyes had consciously included a level of meaning beyond mere narrative, a *sens* to inform their traditional subject matter; but there is nothing to equal the metaphysical reach of the Knight's Tale. The only comparable work is Chaucer's own *Troilus and Criseyde,* and there the inner meaning is given such extensive treatment that the story could almost be seen as an extended *exemplum* of love *versus* mutability. In the *Troilus,* romance is subsumed into tragedy; and the explicit Christianity of the close can only exist beyond the confines of the fiction. In the Knight's Tale Chaucer can find a place for Theseus's affirmation of faith within the structure of the poem. In both poems, however, it is hard to reconcile the ending fully with what has gone before.

The Knight's Tale raises questions; it does not finally answer them. It can ask them quite specifically, as over the rival demerits of imprisonment or exile:

> Yow loveres axe I now this questioun:
> Who hath the worse, Arcite or Palamoun?
>
> (ll. 1347–48)

In a work such as the *Filocolo* such questions are raised precisely in order to be resolved; but Chaucer does not stay to give an answer, any more than he answers Palamon's question about the order underlying the suffering of the innocent, "What governance is in this prescience?" or Arcite's "What is this world?" This refusal to resolve is echoed in the perpetual juxtapositions of joy and grief, brilliant colour and darkness. At the level of style too the Knight's Tale reaches out towards both extremes. Most immediately striking is the high rhetorical formality: the great set pieces of the descriptions of the temples or of the combatants in the tournament, the philosophical declamations, the elaboration of style through figures of speech. Chaucer's use of *occupatio,* the device of describing something under the pretence of refusing to do so, is notorious, and has even been seen as satirical. This is not usually the case: he often uses the device to summarise a section of the *Teseida* that he does not wish to give in full, and the figure can be strikingly effective for conveying a sense of richness of background, as if the poet finds even describing the tip of the iceberg overwhelming. Running in counterpoint to this use of high style, however, is a rougher, more idiomatic use of language that one would expect to be rhetorically indecorous, inappropriate, in an aristocratic romance, but which possesses a deeper decorum appropriate to the greater reach of the Knight's Tale.

Style is keyed very carefully to tone throughout the poem. High style demands, for instance, imagery of a certain level, and up to a point Chaucer fulfills that requirement. It is the lark that announces the dawn, not the more familiar cock that acts as time-keeper to the fabliaux; Palamon and Arcite are compared to the noblest beasts, lion and tiger or boars; Lygurge and Emetreus are accompanied by similarly noble beasts, bulls, an eagle, lions and leopards. Chaucer also, however, draws on a range of more commonplace animals that elsewhere in the *Canterbury Tales* are mentioned only in fabliaux or similarly colloquial stories. These references are always belittling. The drunk mouse and the huddled sheep are intentionally reductive images for the condition of mankind. Arcite's comparison of the cousins' rivalry to dogs fighting for a bone that is snatched away by a kite (ll. 1177–80) is a miniature beast-fable whose drop in style matches their falling away from noble ideals of behaviour. The sheer folly of their fighting for the love of a woman who knows nothing whatsoever about it is brusquely expressed by Theseus in a similarly colloquial image:

> She woot namoore of al this hoote fare,
> By God, than woot a cokkow or an hare!
> (ll. 1809–10)

Cuckoos and hares both have sexual associations: the comparison not only mocks the pretensions of the lovers, it points up how far the cousins' passion is from any practical fulfilment. Such unworldly absolutism demands a little gentle mockery.

Most of these shifts in stylistic and tonal level have a clearly definable function. There are others, however, that are more unsettling, which introduce a note of flippancy when the serious potential of the work would seem to be at its greatest. Emily "caste a freendlich ye" on the triumphant Arcite,

> For wommen, as to speken in comune,
> Thei folwen alle the favour of Fortune.
> (ll. 2681–82)

His injury and death are treated with no rhetorical cushioning of hard facts.

> As blak he lay as any cole or crowe,
> So was the blood yronne in his face,
> (ll. 2692–93)

as if the physical damage lessened his humanity. The description of the corruption of his wound is clinically analytic, and ends with a dismissive shrug:

> Ther Nature wol nat wirche,
> Fare wel phisik! go ber the man to chirche!
> (ll. 2759–60)

The detachment from Arcite as a moral and emotional being is at least useful at this point, for the moment of death is usually the cue for a summing up of a man's life; and that would be an embarrassment here, where such a summary of Arcite would be all but identical to a summary of the still living Palamon. Insistence on the physical detail and the commonplaceness of dying replaces a metaphysical consideration of death, which is given a more forceful expression in Arcite's final lament a few lines later. The destination of his soul is shrugged off in a similarly casual way:

> His spirit chaunged hous and wente ther,
> As I cam nevere, I kan nat tellen wher.
> Therfore I stynte, I nam no divinistre;
> Of soules fynde I nat in this registre.
> (ll. 2809–12)

This is less a refusal to follow the soul of a pagan to hell, or to open a debate on whether good pagans have a different fate, than an insistence on keeping a focus on the earth. The saints' lives can assume an encompassing benevolent supernatural order; but that is precisely what the Knight's Tale has called into question. The lines are unsettling, and they are meant to be. They extend to the narrator the inability of the characters within the story to find in the universe any order perceptible to reason or to human knowledge.

Interjections of this kind are alien to the mode of courtly romance and philosophic seriousness of the rest of the tale; they disturb the perspective that the genre and the stylistic level of the rest of the work suggest. They serve as a useful reminder, therefore, that such a perspective is only relative. Seen from one angle, love may be all-demanding and all-powerful; seen from another, it is mere stupidity. Emily may be defined through the initial description of her as the quintessential heroine of romance, but there may also be a level at which she is no different from women "in comune." Arcite may be given a hero's funeral, but medicine can fail with any man, and, as Egeus points out, there is nothing in the least special or individual about death. It is, at the least, appropriate for the opening tale of the whole work that it should be able to look askance at the perspectives it adopts. If the Knight's Tale sets a standard for the rest, it does not pretend to give a definitive view of the world and those who live in it.

The First Two Poets
of the *Canterbury Tales*

C. David Benson

The first, and perhaps the most striking, literary contrast in the *Canterbury Tales* is that between the Knight's Tale and the Miller's Tale. Every reader feels their difference, and Derek Brewer well expresses one of the givens of Chaucer scholarship when he declares: "The contrast between *The Miller's Tale* and *The Knight's Tale* is very refreshing, and very typical of Chaucer. We turn from 'sentence' to 'solas,' from art in the service of serious conviction to art in the service of fun." The change that Brewer and others have noted is true enough, but more needs to be said: the literary opposition between the first two tales is far more profound, consistent, and deliberate than generally recognized. To begin the *Canterbury Tales,* Chaucer created a dynamic conflict between two completely different kinds of secular poetry. This opening contrast is unlike the mixture of corrupt and sublime poetry in the Pardoner's Tale or the juxtaposition of witty trifle and inert didacticism in Sir Thopas and Melibee. Neither the Knight's Tale nor the Miller's Tale is corrupt art, but rather each, through its own brand of magnificent poetry, reveals a particular truth about the world, and thus each contains both *sentence* and *solaas*. Yet good as they are alone, their triumph is in dialectic. When the tales are read together, they produce a complex literary experience much greater than the sum of their individual parts.

From *Chaucer's Drama of Style: Poetic Variety and Contrast in the* Canterbury Tales. © 1986 by the University of North Carolina Press.

The Dramatic Approach and the Link
between the First Two Tales

Dramatic critics have naturally paid special attention to the drunken Miller's boisterous interruption to demand that he be allowed to "quite" the Knight's Tale (1. 3127, F. N. Robinson, 2d ed.), and they deserve much of the credit for insisting on the opposition between the first two tales. Nevertheless, because the dramatic approach understands the contrast as personal and social rather than artistic, it can identify only the most obvious differences and actually hinders the detailed literary comparisons I shall attempt here. When Paul Ruggiers states that "in tone and attitude, vocabulary and word choice, figure of speech and word play, in genre and philosophy, the two pilgrims stand utterly opposed," he expresses the essence of my argument; but because Ruggiers see the opposition occurring between pilgrims and not poems, he does not develop further his valuable literary insights. As long as the first two tales are regarded as essentially "a dramatic collision of generalized social differences," as one recent critic [Burlin] puts it, discussion of their opposition must remain superficial. Not much can be said about the personal conflict between Knight and Miller because, as with most of the pilgrims, we finally know so little about either. In their eagerness to identify differences of class and temperament, critics often slight the more important poetic quarrel between the opening tales.

As often in the *Canterbury Tales,* the relationship between the first two tales and their tellers, though generally appropriate, is not so close that a different narrator is impossible to imagine. Nothing in the Knight's Tale absolutely conflicts with the pilgrim Knight of the General Prologue, but neither are the similarities especially striking. An epic of ancient chivalry is fitting for the Knight, although we might have expected something more specifically Christian from one who is described less as a courtly hero than as the model of a crusader. There also seems to be some conflict between the story told by the Knight and the views the pilgrim expresses after interrupting the Monk's Tale (fr. 7, ll. 2767–79). The Knight's Tale is a serious philosophical work that does not deny the pain or difficulties of life, whereas the Knight's later words seem to approve only a simple, optimistic kind of literature. Such apparent differences between teller and tale are relatively minor and can be explained away, but at the very least they support the view that a general and nominal relationship between the Knight and his tale is as justified by the text as a detailed and dramatic one.

The Miller's Tale has an even looser relationship to its pilgrim. Although a bawdy tale of deceit and low deeds is appropriate to a thief who speaks mostly of "synne and harlotries" (ll. 560–63), as Chaucer himself suggests just before the tale (ll. 3167–84), the subtle brilliance of the actual poetry comes oddly from the mouth of such a "thikke knarre" (l. 549). The Miller's skill at breaking down doors by running at them with his head is the very opposite of the poem's highly polished art. Although they describe two interesting character types, the portraits of the pilgrim Knight and Miller only hint at the complex artistries of their contrasting tales.

The link between the Knight's Tale and the Miller's Tale— usually called the Miller's Prologue—is much discussed by dramatic critics because it seems to unleash so many personal and class tensions, but the passage is even more valuable for its introduction of literary conflict. The drama of style that is the essence of the *Canterbury Tales* first begins only after the drunken Miller shatters beyond repair the Host's proposed order of telling with the aggression for which he is so well known. The Host intends that the Monk should give the second performance, and a little reflection will make clear how different things would have been if the Monk's Tale actually had followed the Knight's Tale. A certain thematic tension would exist (we have already noted the Knight's objections to the Monk's endless list of tragedies), but the effect on the reader of beginning the collection with two such long and serious works would be oppressive, though not unmedieval. After proposing and deliberately rejecting such a dull beginning, Chaucer turns to the crude Miller to initiate the structure of complex literary contrasts that gives excitement and meaning to the *Canterbury Tales*. Despite the Reeve's fear that he will hear nothing better than "lewed dronken harlotrye" (l. 3145) from such a ruffian, the skilled art of the Miller's Tale is the equal, if also the opposite, of the Knight's Tale. Now that the "male" is finally "unbokeled" (l. 3115), what had threatened to become a dreary "game" is truly "wel bigonne" (l. 3117).

The dramatic dispute in the first link signals a deeper artistic conflict between two kinds of poetry. The Knight and the Miller never actually quarrel (or even address a single word to one another), for Robin's challenge is more literary than personal. He declares that his tale, too, will be "noble" and insists that it will not merely follow, but actually "quite" the Knight's Tale (l. 3127). Although the drunken Miller, who can barely sit on his horse, is portrayed as a burlesque of the Knight, the tale he tells is much more than a mocking parody of a superior work. The fabliau uses many of the same literary materials as the romance for different, but equally valuable, purposes. There may be many a "bettre man" (l. 3130) than the churlish Miller, but few poems in or out of the Canterbury collection are superior to the Miller's Tale. It requites the Knight's Tale, as promised, not by discrediting the former work, but by providing a completely different literary experience.

The First Two Poets of the *Canterbury Tales*

As the link between them suggests, the key to understanding the first two Canterbury tales is our recognition of their dynamic literary contrast. Chaucer's initial juxtaposition of an idealistic chivalric romance and a witty tale of sex and deceit, which defines two extremes of secular literature, is more surprising, and deliberately so, than the variety found in other collections of stories such as Ovid's *Metamorphoses* or Boccaccio's *Decameron*. The artistic individuality of the first two tales goes far deeper than their obvious difference in genre: the Knight's Tale has a plain earnestness and philosophical ambition lacking in most continental romances (including its source in Boccaccio's *Teseida*), whereas the Miller's Tale is one of the most ornate fabliaux ever written. The contrast becomes still more interesting when we realize how many elements of the two stories are complementary. Critics have long noticed that the Miller's Tale parallels the Knight's Tale in such things as character, situation, and structure: for instance, a courtly love triangle in the romance is followed by an earthier threesome in the fabliau and lordly Theseus as patriarch is replaced by silly John the carpenter. The tales demand comparison because of their different handling of shared elements, a comparison that reveals the individual poetic sensibility and worldview at work in each. In length, characterization, word choice, imagery, speech—whichever element we care to look at—the first two Canterbury tales, though equally impressive, are radically and consistently opposed. At the very beginning of the *Canterbury Tales* Chaucer introduces an extreme example of the literary contrast that will distinguish the entire work.

The contrasting artistries of the Knight's Tale and the Miller's Tale announce themselves from the first. The direct yet magnificent art of the romance appears within its opening five lines:

> Whilom, as olde stories tellen us,
> Ther was a duc that highte Theseus;
> Of Atthenes he was lord and governour.
> And in his tyme swich a conquerour,
> That gretter was ther noon under the sonne.
>
> (ll. 859–63)

Although its style and vocabulary are relatively simple, the passage moves with a leisurely stateliness that is appropriate to the tale's exalted themes. In the first line we learn that the subject is not only ancient, but also popular enough so that several stories (note the plural) have already been told about it. Theseus is introduced by name, a name (along with that of the famous city of Athens) that is both familiar and impressive to the reader. Theseus is then assigned a series of titles ("lord," "governour," and "conquerour"); although the terms themselves are not uncommon, they suggest power and control and are suitably grand without being grandiose. The phrase "lord and governour" in the third line is typical of the many doublets found throughout the poem. While redundant and thus not strictly necessary for sense, such phrases, like the equally superfluous "and in his tyme" in the next line, give dignity to the narration while contributing to its slow, careful development. The image with which the quotation ends, "That gretter was ther noon under the sonne," is, like the passage as a whole, both simple and magnificent. "Under the sonne" is another redundancy, but it hints at the scope of the poem, which deals with both heaven and earth, and it is thus an appropriately lordly image with which to describe Theseus.

When we turn to the beginning of the Miller's Tale, its contrasting poetic is immediately apparent:

> Whilom ther was dwellynge at Oxenford
> A riche gnof, that gestes heeld to bord,
> And of his craft he was a carpenter.
> With hym ther was dwellynge a poure scoler,

> Hadde lerned art, but al his fantasye
> Was turned for to lerne astrologye.
>
> (ll. 3187–92)

Although the fabliau opens with the same word as the romance and also immediately describes the oldest male character in the story, its style is very different. Unlike the steadily developed grandeur of the Knight's Tale, the first lines of the Miller's contain a series of anticlimaxes and frustrated expectations. The story takes place in Oxford, but the first character is not an academic. The churl is rich, but he takes in boarders; and though he has a craft, it is the fairly low one of carpenter. The scholar, for his part, has been educated in the liberal arts, but his real interest is in astrology. The opening account of Theseus in the Knight's Tale magnified his importance until he seemed little less than the sun, but description of character here is deliberately reductive. For instance, the term "gnof" is in striking contrast to the noble titles given the romance hero: used nowhere else by Chaucer, and, according to the *Middle English Dictionary*, nowhere else in Middle English, it is clearly a comic, even insulting label, so that the phrase "riche gnof" is probably meant to be somewhat oxymoronic.

In contrast to the dignified and smooth opening of the Knight's Tale, the narration here shifts quickly from the unnamed carpenter, who is nominally head of household, to the unnamed scholar, making us wonder, as we do not in the romance, who is to be the central character and who will dominate. Theseus is clearly established as a figure of accomplishment and control from the beginning of the tale, but the effect of the first lines of the fabliau is conflict and tension. Whereas the simple dignity at the beginning of the Knight's Tale suggests the coherence of its world, the Miller's Tale opens with a series of sharp oppositions (rich versus poor, landlord versus tenant, town versus gown, study versus play, and, implicitly, old versus young) whose instability will be exploited during the rest of the tale for comic effect. The sharp contrast of these initial passages first announces the individual sensibilities and values of the two poems.

The different kinds of art that Chaucer has given to each of the first two tales determine what we see and how we see it, even when the events described are superficially similar. A good example is the marriage mentioned early in each tale. The account of Theseus's conquest of the Amazons and subsequent marriage to their queen, Hippolyta (ll. 866–85), contains the same direct, dignified poetry found in the opening lines of the tale. Although the passage uses many exalted words, such as "glorie," "solempnytee," "victorie," "noble," and "chivalrye," and deals with extraordinary events, the style is relatively simple and unadorned: for example, "He conquered al the regne of Femenye, / That whilom was ycleped Scithia, / And weddede the queene Ypolita" (ll. 866–68). If the passage reads like the voice of sober historical truth, this is in part because the verse is devoid of concrete imagery, similes, or literary allusion. The most noticeable literary device in the passage is *occupatio*, which introduces an authoritative but friendly narrative voice ("And certes, if it nere to long to heere" [l. 875]), which both asserts the scope of the story (so extensive that it must be cut short) and demonstrates an ability to manage such rich material. The solid artistry of the Knight's Tale allows it to deal with large and even symbolic subjects (a great war between Athens and the Amazons and, implicitly, the right relationship between men and women), while maintaining a clear, coherent narrative. Order is celebrated in the Knight's Tale and illustrated by the poet's sure control, although the many difficulties of this world, from war to the hostile weather during the couple's return, are not ignored.

The first mention of the much less successful marriage between John and Alisoun in the Miller's Tale just as surely defines its special poetry (ll. 3221–32). The courtship and wedding are dismissed in a single line, and the focus is instead on the couple's life together afterward—an almost certain guarantee of comedy rather than romance. The marriage is less noble in the Miller's Tale than in the Knight's Tale, and the verse employs a greater variety of literary devices in fewer lines. Unlike the romance account, the fabliau passage contains vigorous imagery and even a literary allusion to Cato. Alisoun is likened to an animal held "narwe in cage" who yet remains "wylde," suggesting that, in contrast to the ultimately harmonious union in the romance, the natural impulses of the wife in this tale are unwillingly constrained: an unstable and thus potentially comic situation. The marriage of Theseus and Hippolyta can be seen as an emblem of personal and political order; but precisely because we are invited to read the couple symbolically, they remain rather vague as human beings. In contrast, the wedded pair in the Miller's Tale is more rooted in physical and psychological reality. We are told Alisoun's exact age and John's fear of cuckoldry. A final difference is that the narrative voice in the second passage is less pleasant; it remains distant, giving no sign that it is in any way shaping the story, and draws a lesson that offers not comfort but only a cool determinism: "He moste endure, as oother folk, his care" (l. 3232). No reader of Chaucer will be surprised to learn that marriage in the Miller's Tale is described differently from marriage in the Knight's Tale, but detailed comparison reveals that the obvious clash of two genres extends farther than we would expect, to the smallest particulars of style.

Other parallel scenes in the first two tales also contribute to defining their contrasting poets. For example, each tale contains an unexpected physical catastrophe near the end of its story: the fatal fall of Arcite from his horse (ll. 2671–2966) and the ridiculous fall of old John from the rafters when he thinks Noah's flood has come (ll. 3816–49). In its elaborate account of the consequences of Arcite's fall, the romance combines narrative action, moving speeches by several characters, and detailed reports of exotic funeral ceremonies to produce a powerful pageant of heroic death that contrasts sharply to the fabliau's clever mix of rapid action and dialogue to depict silly John's hurt and humiliation. Recognition of these artistic differences enables us to see the poetry of each tale more clearly, and this leads to larger thematic differences: the Knight's Tale takes Arcite's death very seriously and tries to find meaning in it, whereas the Miller's Tale with its funny and cruel narrative climax, turns all John's "harm unto a jape" (l. 3842).

The first two Canterbury tales are conspicuous examples of poetry that calls special attention to the way in which it is told. In both tales a close connection exists between artistry and meaning, so that art itself becomes an important theme in each. Critics of the Miller's Tale have long been aware of the flamboyant skill of its imagery, elaborate character portraits, parodies, and puns. The deliberate art of the Knight's Tale, so obvious in its opening lines, has also been recognized by many. In his influential essay on the first tale, Charles Muscatine stresses the importance of its artificial style and balanced structure, which does not aim to represent real life, but instead produces a "poetic pageant" concerned with ceremony, ritual, and the creation of order. Robert Jordan suggests a direct link between the style of this romance and its philosophical ideas and, in an approach recently echoed by others, shows that "the idea of form itself becomes a major theme" of the tale, thus forcing the reader to examine closely the poet's own art.

The artistic self-consciousness of the first two tales is seen most clearly in an element both share: a major character who functions as an artist-figure within the story. Theseus, who works to establish harmony and order, plays this role in the Knight's Tale, while Nicholas, an instigator of deceit and confusion, does so in the Miller's. Once he has conquered the Amazons and Creon, Theseus often seems as much a humanist, or at least a patron, as a warrior; in addition to his vast building projects, he is a rhetorician of love and philosophy and the generous impresario of noble ceremonies that include the chivalric tournament and Arcite's funeral. Nicholas is a very different but equally accomplished artist, whose talents extend far beyond his musical skills and general handiness; he arranges the dumb show in his room that alarms the carpenter and is a gifted storyteller, as his account of the coming flood proves. In their separate ways of converting the stuff of life into art, Theseus and Nicholas epitomize the poetic method of each tale.

Each of the two artist-figures creates a construction that is central to the plot of his poem and also defines its special artistry. In the Knight's Tale the revealing artifact is Theseus's "noble theatre" (l. 1885)—which in Boccaccio's *Teseida* is not built for the occasion but already exists—a perfectly round structure of simple but harmonious beauty, which takes on great symbolic signifcance. The stadium expresses the theme of the tale as well as its art: like the romance as a whole, it does not deny that the universe contains malevolent forces (seen primarily in the baleful influence of the pagan gods), but attempts to contain and rationalize them. Both the stadium and the Knight's Tale are attempts to produce harmony and even love out of human conflict, though the success of each is limited. Almost at the beginning of its description, we are told that the stadium is "ful of degrees" (l. 1890). Although this phrase really means little more than that the theater had many rows of seats, it perfectly describes the romance as a whole, which deals with degree in the widest sense—the right ordering of both human society and the universe, especially as expressed in Theseus's speech on the divine Chain of Love. The stadium is said to be built so that "whan a man was set on o degree, / He letted nat his felawe for to see" (ll. 1891–92), a good analogy to the clear and direct art of the Knight's Tale itself. Yet within this symbolically round structure are also the many intricate carvings and paintings that decorate the temples of the gods (ll. 1914–17), a reminder of the complex literary skill beneath the deliberate simplicity of the tale, just as the often terrible events described in the temples reflect the work's serious, even tragic themes.

The corresponding artistic construct in the Miller's Tale is the tubs that Nicholas persuades John to hang in anticipation of a new flood. These homely and somewhat ridiculous objects may seem insignificant in comparison with a grand amphitheater, but they accurately represent the different, but not inferior, art of the fabliau. Although presented more briefly than Theseus's noble theater, the tubs are given a physical solidity and precision lacking in the romance account of the building of the lists: we see John collecting and hanging the three different kinds ("knedyng trogh," "tubbe," and "kymelyn"), making a ladder to reach them, climbing up "by the ronges and the stalkes," and stocking them with bread, cheese, and "good ale in a jubbe" (ll. 3620–29). The art of the Knight's Tale is more idealistic and philosophical, but the Miller's Tale conveys a better sense of the tangible objects and actual processes of this world. The tubs also accurately reflect the cleverness, deceit, and fun of the fabliau. Nicholas devises a cruel trap—so elaborate that it suggests love of inventiveness for its own sake—that he gets the victim himself to set. Hanging high in the rafters and containing a profoundly ignorant man, the tubs create a delicious tension in the reader, who, even if momentarily diverted by other events, knows that what has gone up must inevitably come crashing down to John's sorrow and our delight.

THE ARTISTIC DIALECTIC OF THE FIRST TWO TALES

The individual, contrasting artistries of the first two tales—symbolized by the differences between Theseus and Nicholas and their two constructs—is found at all levels and throughout each work. The frequent resort in the Knight's Tale to doublets that slow down the verse while giving it greater dignity, already mentioned and another manifestation of the balance and symmetry that is the essence of the poem, is very much the opposite of the puns, double entendres, and clever rhymes in the Miller's Tale. In contrast to the well-known physical solidity and precise descriptions of the Miller's Tale, which need no further illustration here, the abstract Knight's Tale often ignores the everyday world and instead presents a significant number of ceremonies (funerals, weddings, tournaments, feasts) and symbolic events. Even when the Knight's Tale is most vivid, as in its accounts of the sculpture and paintings of the three pagan temples, the poetry often remains in the service of allegorical abstraction, as in this famous example: "The pykepurs, and eek the pale Drede; / The smylere with the knyf under the cloke" (ll. 1998–99).

Valuable as it is to recognize these general differences, only a detailed comparison between specific literary elements, like the one tentatively offered in the following pages, can begin to reveal the full depth and consistency of the artistic contrast in the first two tales. The special poetic achievements (and limitations) of each are seen most clearly when the two tales are read together, one in the light of the other, as their juxtaposition invites. Such a dialectic demonstrates the individual poetic of both the Knight's Tale and the Miller's Tale (though any specific conclusion may be rejected or modified by others), confirming the proverbial wisdom of Pandarus in *Troilus and Criseyde:* "By his contrarie is every thyng declared" (l. 637).

Narrative Voice

Our brief comparison of a marriage in each of the first two tales revealed a contrast between the involved narrator of the Knight's Tale and the cool, somewhat contemptuous narrator of the Miller's Tale—a difference that is consistently developed throughout each poem. I should at once make clear that in the following discussion I am restricting the term "narrator." When using the word, I am not referring to the general exposition of the tale (that is the product of what I call the "poet"), but only to those specific passages in which the narrative voice intrudes to speak directly to the audience.

The authoritative, conscientious, and at times even warm voice of the narrator of the Knight's Tale is frequently heard throughout the romance. Ruling the tale as firmly as Theseus does Athens, it shapes, controls, and attempts to bring order out of confusion. The narrator's self-conscious manipulation of his material is evident from the very beginning of the story. Within the first twenty lines, in the only passage that refers specifically to the larger tale-telling contest, he says that if it were not "to long to heere" (l. 875), he would tell us of the battle and wedding between Theseus and Hippolyta, but "I have, God woot, a large feeld to ere, / And wayke been the oxen in my plough" (ll. 886–87). This *occupatio* is the first of many in the tale: a major shaping device of the narrative voice that allows it, as Muscatine shows, "to shorten the story without lessening its weight and impressiveness."

The narrator's control of his material is also revealed by the care with which he makes transitions. Because of its vast scope, the romance must often move between different locales or characters, and when it does the narrator goes out of his way to inform the reader of what is happening. One example that will have to stand for several others (my own *occupatio*) is an early transition from one of the lovers to the other:

> Now wol I stynte of Palamon a lite,
> And lete hym in his prisoun stille dwelle,
> And of Arcita forth I wol yow telle.
>
> (ll. 1334–36)

Assertions of narrative authority such as *occupatio* and careful transitions not only define the special narrative voice of the Knight's Tale but also reflect the themes of order and responsibility in the tale as a whole.

If the narrator of the Knight's Tale takes conspicuous command of his tale, he is no fierce and distant ruler. Although many of the events in the romance are strange and glorious, as befits such an ancient, heroic tale, the narrator's voice is remarkably personal. He often uses the pronoun "I" and is engaged with both his characters and readers to a degree unprecedented in Boccaccio's *Teseida*. When Arcite is freed from prison on the condition that he never return to Troy, the narrator comments, "Lat hym be war! his nekke lith to wedde" (l. 1218); when the same knight lies fatally wounded, the narrator bursts out, "Fare wel phisik! go ber the man to chirche!" (l. 2760). The narrator easily admits his limitations as a versifier (ll. 1459–61) and theologian (ll. 2809–14), and, like Theseus, though often formal, he can also be rustically proverbial: "Now in the crope, now doun in the breres, / Now up, now doun, as boket in a welle" (ll. 1532–33).

The audience (or at least the lovers in it) is directly addressed at the end of the first section (ll. 1347–54) and is throughout spoken to in conversational, even friendly tones: for example, "Ther as the

knyghtes weren in prisoun / Of which I tolde yow and tellen shal"
(ll. 1058–59). The longest formal set piece in the poem, the account
of the three pagan temples, is made more intimate and vivid by
narrative involvement. The voice first ingenuously claims to have
forgotten to describe the oratories (ll. 1914–17), and then says that
he would like to tell everything about the portraits ("Why sholde I
noght as wel eek telle yow al / The portreiture that was upon the
wal" [ll. 1967–68]), even though that is impossible ("I may nat
rekene hem alle though I wolde" [l. 2040]). He dramatizes the
sights in the temples by constantly repeating "ther saugh I" or a
similiar phrase (for example, ll. 1995, 2005, 2011, 2017, 2028, 2056,
2062, 2067, and 2073).

The careful but kindly narrator of the Knight's Tale, whom the
reader both likes and trusts, is strikingly different from the imper-
sonal, often contemptuous narrator of the Miller's Tale, who delights in the foolishness of his character as much as the reader does.
A direct narrative voice is rarely heard in the Miller's Tale, whose
action is generally allowed to unfold quickly without the exterior
comment that would get in the way of its comedy. In contrast to
the romance, narrative transitions in the fabliau are either brief
("Now, sire, and eft, sire, so bifel the cas" [l. 3271]) or so smooth
that they are hardly noticed, as when we go from the initial
description of Absolon in church to an account of his wooing that
evening: "The moone, whan it was nyght, ful brighte shoon" (l.
3352). The brisk style of narration forces the reader directly into the
action of the story, so that often the only indication of transition
from one scene to another is an insistent demonstrative—"this
parissh clerk, this amorous Absolon" (l. 3657) or "this Nicholas" (l.
3798). Such is the form of one of the most dazzling transitions in all
literature, when, after the searing of Nicholas and his anguished
cry, we suddenly return to the all-but-forgotten John in his tub:

> This carpenter out of his slomber sterte,
> And herde oon crien "water" as he were wood,
> And thoughte, "Allas, now comth Nowelis flood!"
>
> (ll. 3816–18)

The few first-person statements in the Miller's Tale are perfunctory and not at all personal: for example, "I dar wel seyn" (l.
3346) or "as I gesse" (l. 3644). In contrast to the friendly, informa-

tive *occupatio* in the Knight's Tale, expressions of abbreviation in the Miller's Tale are simply curt ("I may nat rekene hem alle" [l. 3198] or "as I have told biforn" [l. 3302]) and never indicate the slightest affection for the characters or audience. When the narrator notices the former at all, his response is either noncommittal ("Now ber thee wel, thou hende Nicholas" [l. 3397]) or infinitely superior, as when John is alarmed for his wife's safety: "Lo, which a greet thyng is affeccioun!" (l. 3611). The last words of the narrator in the Knight's Tale warmly address both the happiness of Palamon and Emelye and the audience ("And God save al this faire compaignye" [ll. 3097–3108], but when the fabliau narrator reappears at the end of his tale, it is to offer a smug, heartless, and wonderfully funny summing up:

> Thus swyved was this carpenteris wyf,
> For al his kepyng and his jalousye;
> And Absolon hath kist hir nether ye;
> And Nicholas is scalded in the towte.
> This tale is doon, and God save al the rowte!
>
> (ll. 3850–54)

The contrasting narrators of the first two tales are a function of the different kinds of poetry Chaucer has created for each work and should not be closely associated with the nominal tellers. Although the serious, kindly narrator of the Knight's Tale seems generally (but not much more than generally) similar to the pilgrim Knight, the cool, superior narrator of the Miller's Tale is nothing like the drunken Miller. Nor are the different narrators simply a result of genre. Medieval romances of the ancient past often have a less personally involved, more formal narrative voice than we find in the Knight's Tale, the most relevant example being its immediate source—Boccaccio's *Teseida*. The narrator in Chaucer's other long classical romance, *Troilus and Criseyde*, though even more prominent, has a very different voice (more nervous and bookish, for example) than the one heard here. Correspondingly, the narrative voice often plays a much greater role in other fabliaux than it does in the Miller's Tale, as we shall soon see in Chaucer's own Reeve's Tale and Merchant's Tale. As is best realized, through the dialectic of comparison, Chaucer has given each of the narrators in his first two tales a unique and highly effective voice.

Character Portraits

The extreme change in genre from romance to fabliau in the first two tales inevitably results in two sets of characters unlike one another in class, manners, values, and interests. More revealing than these inevitable, objective differences, however, is the significant contrast between the way each poet chooses to present his characters in formal description. The method of characterization, as distinct from the characters themselves, is unique to each tale and another indication of the deep and consistent artistic conflict at the beginning of the *Canterbury Tales*.

The principal women of the two tales, Emelye and Alisoun, provide the most obvious illustration of each poet's approach. The characterization of Emelye in the Knight's Tale is simple and idealized, as the opening lines of her description reveal:

> Till it fil ones, in a morwe of May,
> That Emelye, that fairer was to sene
> Than is the lylie upon his stalke grene,
> And fressher than the May with floures newe—
> For with the rose colour stroof hire hewe,
> I noot which was the fyner of hem two.
>
> (ll. 1034–39)

The images of May, rose, and lily are common and associate the heroine with a traditional type of romance heroine. They are not meant to individualize or vivify her. The leisurely passage, which goes on for sixteen more lines to describe Emelye's yellow hair and angel's voice, is clear and straightforward, but, in contrast to her portrait in the *Teseida*, allows us to see Emelye, even when she walks before us, only as a distant ideal.

The characterization of Alisoun in the Miller's Tale proceeds from a deliberately different, though equally skillful, literary sensibility. Alisoun is described in a long and elaborate portrait (ll. 3233–70) so famous that I shall quote only a few lines from the end:

> A brooch she baar upon hir lowe coler,
> As brood as is the boos of a bokeler.
> Her shoes were laced on hir legges hye.
> She was a prymerole, a piggesnye,
> For any lord to leggen in his bedde,
> Or yet for any good yeman to wedde.
>
> (ll. 3265–70)

In contrast to the romance portrait, what we are told about Alisoun is specific and physical. Although generally objective, the poet is capable of sudden, revealing thrusts: "And sikerly she hadde a likerous ye" (l. 3244). The most original quality of this portrait, however, is the concentration of vivid imagery whose effect is comically reductive rather than idealizing. Alisoun is associated with a series of rustic images (such as milk, sheep's wool, apples) and likened not to a lily or rose but to a "piggesnye," which, as Donaldson has shown, if a flower, also "remains, unmistakably, a pig's eye." Although we never see Alisoun perform any real action, the method of characterization—which links her with several frisky animals (including a weasel, swallow, calf, kid, and colt), while emphasizing her active look, shining hue, and playful skipping— produces a lively, tangible woman, to whom we do not respond as we did to Emelye. The poet involves the reader with Alisoun as a physical and sexually attractive creature by reminding us of the body beneath her clothes and even turning her around for our inspection.

The different method of characterization in each of the first two tales is not dictated by their separate genres. Although largely absent from the Knight's Tale, detailed, physical description of major characters, especially women, is a common feature of medieval romance, the most obvious examples of which are found throughout *Troilus and Criseyde*. Correspondingly, the average fabliau, far from containing elaborate portraits like that of Alisoun, relies on quite perfunctory character description of the kind found in Chaucer's own Shipman's Tale. Critics have long recognized that Chaucer greatly altered the characterization he found in the sources for his first two tales. The principal figures in the Knight's Tale, with the exception of Theseus, are less vivid and individualized than their models in Boccaccio's *Teseida*, whereas the complex portraits of Nicholas, Alisoun, and Absolon are almost certainly Chaucer's contribution to the Miller's Tale. What has not been stressed is the extreme contrast. Chaucer's changes in the first two tales, though not demanded by genre, are in exactly opposite directions—from significantly less detailed characterization in the Knight's Tale to significantly more detailed characterization in the Miller's Tale. The unique poetry of each tale is once again seen most clearly when the two works are read closely together.

Although neither of the first two Canterbury tales describes all its characters in exactly the same way, each has its own special approach, which remains consistent throughout the work. Characterization in the Knight's Tale is symbolic, distant, and ideal, whereas that in the Miller's Tale is ironically reductive, local, and helpful to the plot. The difference is perhaps best seen in the contrast between secondary rather than major characters: Absolon in the fabliau and the two champions, Lygurge and Emetreus, in the romance.

On the surface at least, the long portraits of Lygurge and Emetreus (ll. 2128–89), constructed with great care from accounts of many different warriors in Boccaccio, seem unlike the description of Emelye and closer to the detailed characterization of the Miller's Tale. Looked at more closely, however, especially in direct comparison with the fabliau, it is clear that the form of the portraits, like that of characterization elsewhere in the Knight's Tale, is essentially emblematic. By this I mean that, although the champions add to the splendor of the poetic pageant and reflect its concern with balance and symmetry, neither is essential to the plot, and the considerable information provided in their portraits is never referred to again. As with Emelye, the champions are not seen as individuals, but rather as traditional types. Both heroes are described in an objective, rather stiff style, without irony or insinuation, that is closer to the conventional medieval catalogue portrait than character description elsewhere in Chaucer, including the General Prologue. The portrait of Emetreus, for example, begins with a general view and then moves from his hair to his nose, to his eyes, to his lips, to his complexion, to his beard, to his voice, to his head as a whole, to his hand, and, finally, to what is around him.

The long portrait of Absolon in the Miller's Tale has its own ornateness, but one in the service of an entirely different poetic. Its function is not emblematic but practical. Absolon's vanity (ll. 3314–16), personal fastidiousness (ll. 3319–24), involvement in non-religious activities (ll. 3325–30), music making (ll. 3331–33), flirtations among the lower classes (ll. 3334–36), and dislike of farting (ll. 3337–38) will all be used in the plot of the Miller's Tale. Even the surprising detail that his eyes are as "greye as goos" exactly defines the clerk's difference from the genuine courtly lover (l. 3317): the usual phrase in the romances is "gray as glass," but Absolon is, indeed, a silly goose and the change accurately predicts his amatory incompetence. In contrast to the exotic descriptions of the pagan heroes in the Knight's Tale, which contribute to the noble tone of the romance, the portrait of Absolon is made familiar by the use of ordinary and parochial details, any one of which is impossible to imagine in the Knight's Tale: the windows of St. Paul's, a *kirtel*, shoelaces, a surplice, a land charter, a *rubible*, a *giterne*, and a tavern (ll. 3318–34). The difference from characterization in the Knight's Tale goes beyond genre; other fabliaux, even those by Chaucer, contain nothing like this profusion of specific detail.

The different kinds of characterization in the first two tales require opposite responses from the reader. We have every reason to trust the heroic portraits of Lygurge and Emetreus in the Knight's Tale, but the description of the "myrie child" in the Miller's Tale contains so much satire and ironic comment that we cannot accept it at face value. The reader must alertly interpret the portrait, discovering for himself (because the narrative stance is so disingenuously admiring) the implications of such things as Absolon's biblical name, his hair and dress, and his many secular pursuits. Not that the Miller's Tale demands more from the reader than the Knight's Tale (responding to the ancient and ideal is also difficult), but its demands are radically different. The characterizations of the pagan champions and of Absolon are each excellent and appropriate to their individual works.

Speech

Because it is uttered by the characters themselves, direct speech cannot easily be attributed to the pilgrim tellers and is thus rarely discussed in dramatic interpretations of the *Canterbury Tales*. Nevertheless, the different use of speech in the first two tales is an essential part of their opposing artistries and can tell us much about the two poets. The formal, often quite serious and emotional monologues that are characteristic of the Knight's Tale are nothing like the rapid, witty dialogue found throughout the Miller's Tale. The significant difference between speech in these tales once again goes beyond genre. Chaucer's other romance set in ancient times, *Troilus and Criseyde,* has much more variety of speech than the Knight's Tale, just as his other fabliaux, especially the Shipman's Tale and the Merchant's Tale, contain more formal and extended speech than anything in the Miller's Tale.

The different kinds of speech in the first two tales are clear from the first spoken words in each. Although the opening speech in the romance, which is given by Theseus, is an angry demand to know why the ladies in black have disturbed his homecoming, his words remain elevated and carefully balanced:

> "What folk been ye, that at myn homcomynge
> Perturben so my feste with criynge?"
> Quod Theseus. "Have ye so greet envye
> Of myn honour, that thus compleyne and crye?
> Or who hath yow mysboden or offended?
> And telleth me if it may been amended,
> And why that ye been clothed thus in blak."
>
> (ll. 905–11)

In response, the eldest of the grieving widows delivers a long speech whose rhetorical intricacy does not exclude either literary brilliance or deep feeling (ll. 915–47).

Compare this formal but emotional exchange in the romance with the opening spoken words in the Miller's Tale: the vivacious, tricky, and quite insincere dialogue between Nicholas and Alisoun, which cleverly uses courtly parody to produce a magnificent juxtaposition of act and utterance:

> [Nicholas] seyde, "Ywis, but if ich have my wille,
> For deerne love of thee, lemman, I spille."
> And heeld hire harde by the haunchebones,
> And seyde, "Lemman, love me al atones,
> Or I wol dyen, also God me save!"
> And she sproong as a colt dooth in the trave,
> And with hir heed she wryed faste awey,
> And seyde, "I wol nat kisse thee, by my fey!
> Why, lat be," quod she, "lat be, Nicholas,
> Or I wol crie 'out, harrow' and 'allas'!
> Do wey youre handes, for youre curteisye!"
>
> (ll. 3277–87)

These contrasting kinds of speech remain consistent throughout the two tales. When Palamon first catches sight of Emelye, he initially utters only a single syllable—"A" (l. 1078)—but he and Arcite soon deliver three relatively long, formal speeches on love and fortune, whose earnestness may provoke a smile from the reader (ll. 1081–1111 and 1118–22). Then, after one of the few examples of dialogue in the poem (ll. 1125–27), the knights deliver an additional pair of even longer speeches on the subject of who should love Emelye (ll. 1129–86). The poet has no desire to make the words of the rivals sound realistic, nor does he distinguish between them; as with speeches in Thucydides or classical drama, these lines are to be read as heightened presentations of the characters' thoughts and general position rather than as actual expressions.

The speeches of Theseus, the central character in the Knight's Tale, are similarly abstract and thematically important. When Theseus comes upon Palamon and Arcite fighting in the wood, the poet reveals his hero's changing will through a series of deliberately stylized utterances. Theseus first angrily pronounced a death sentence against the two knights (ll. 1743–47), which prompts Hippolyta and Emelye to offer a courtly plea for mercy (l. 1757). After considering the request seriously (for speech in the Knight's Tale can persuade the noble to good action as the widows of the Theban warriors have already learned), Theseus utters an address on the need for mercy in a lord, which is no less formal for being addressed to himself (ll. 1773–81). The noble duke then gives a long discourse on the comedy of love (ll. 1785–1825)—perhaps the most amusing and rhetorically skilled speech on love ever delivered by a political ruler on horseback—which is followed, once the two knights pray for mercy, with an ex tempore, yet comprehensive and well-organized, statement describing the tournament he will arrange to decide who shall marry Emelye (ll. 1829–69). Of course, none of these utterances sounds much like real speech, for that is not their purpose; instead, they carefully, if perhaps a bit too schematically, define an ideal of the just and sensitive ruler.

Speech in the Knight's Tale, while frequently passionate and never obscure, is always elevated and thoughtful, as befits a poem so deeply concerned with crucial matters like order, justice, and man's relation to the cosmos. Even when the young knights are most smitten by their love for Emelye, they nevertheless talk philosophically of fate and fortune, just as Theseus's witty meditation on the folly of love makes an important point about the limitations of this world, and Arcite's last, deeply emotional words remain rhetorically sophisticated and in control despite his imminent death (ll. 2765–97). The final long speech in the poem is Theseus's magnificent First Mover speech, which puts all that has happened in a divine context of harmony and love, while also bringing about the marriage of Palamon and Emelye to strengthen the political union between Thebes and Athens (ll. 2987–3093).

In contrast to the formal, persuasive, and often philosophical discourses of the Knight's Tale, speech in the Miller's Tale is tricky, manipulative, and intended primarily to deceive. Like the poem as a whole, the characters create elaborate, witty fictions full of tricks and surprises. In addition to its frequent cruelty and clever deceit, talk in the Miller's Tale is impressively colloquial and individualistic. As opposed to the romance in which everyone sounds alike, the fabliau uses speech to characterize its actors. Although "Tehee" may be Alisoun's most famous utterance (l. 3740), her earthy directness and shrewdness are apparent in all her words, just as the dim credulousness of John is confirmed every time he opens his mouth. The poet is also skilled enough to distinguish Nicholas's artful appropriation of courtly language to soften the directness of his wooing ("Lemman, love me al atones, / Or I wol dyen, also God me save!" [ll. 3280–81]) from Absolon's ludicrous incompetence with the same idiom, such as his description of himself as a sweaty animal yearning for its mother's milk (ll. 3700–3704).

The only extended speech in the Miller's Tale—Nicholas's warning to John of the new flood (l. 3501–3600)—though just as long as some of the monologues in the Knight's Tale, is very different from their abstract, rhetorically elevated style. Nicholas's exposition is broken up by questions and answers, by constant reminders (as almost never occur in the romance) that one person is actually speaking to another (for example, "as I have seyd" [l. 3567] or "be wel avysed" [l. 3584]), and even by a quotation of what will be said in the future [ll. 3577–80]). The actual monologue on the flood is dramatically introduced by a lively dialogue between John and Nicholas in which the student excites both his landlord and the reader with a dramatic opening statement ("Allas! / Shal al the world be lost eftsoones now?" [ll. 3488–89]) and with his promise to tell secrets (ll. 3493–95). Indeed, in his vivacious fabrication of the apocalyptic flood, Nicholas proves that his powers of storytelling equal those of the Miller-poet himself.

Allusions, Imagery, and Vocabulary

The artistic dialectic of the first two Canterbury tales occurs throughout and on all levels: smaller elements, such as learned allusions, imagery, and vocabulary, further demonstrate the extent and consistency of the contrasting poetic voices. In one of the few literary, as opposed to dramatic, comparisons that have been attempted between the Knight's Tale and the Miller's Tale, Christopher Dean shows that the imagery in each has different functions and almost never uses the same objects. For example, Dean notes that animal imagery in the fabliau draws on the familiar beasts of the English countryside in contrast to the exotic lions, tigers, griffins, and eagles of the romance. These findings accord with what we have previously learned about the poets of each tale: imagery in the Miller's Tale serves primarily to "describe people from the outside" and then "the physical world in which they live," whereas imagery in the Knight's Tale "deals primarily with abstract ideas and people's emotions." Dean's conclusions are especially valuable because they are based on such detailed comparisons, but other elements in the first two tales are equally revealing.

Neither the Knight's Tale nor the Miller's is as bookish as many of Chaucer's other works, yet their use of learned and literary allusion, even within these limits, is significantly different. Given the subject of the Knight's Tale, we are not surprised that it contains mythological stories, classical figures like Fortune and Phoebus, and frequent mention of the pagan gods, often as planetary deities. Despite this degree of ancient coloring, however, Chaucer has severely reduced the amount of classical material and allusions he found in Boccaccio's *Teseida*. The poet's interests are not particularly literary. Aside from a long, unacknowledged use of Boethius's *Consolation of Philosophy* in Theseus's First Mover speech, which adds philosophical weight to the tale whatever its limitations, most of the learning in the poem is historical and factual (at least by medieval standards): in addition to mythological stories (see also a reference to Hector at line 2832), the poem contains some exotic classical lore, such as the "opie of Thebes fyn" (l. 1472), and details of ancient religious and funeral rites. For all its genuine interest in the past, references in the Knight's Tale to other literary texts are perfunctory. A quotation on the lawlessness of lovers is identified only as an "olde clerkes sawe" (l. 1163), though many manuscripts note in the margin that it is actually from Boethius, and no specific source is mentioned for the story of Perotheus except for a vague reference to "olde books" (ll. 1191–1200; see also ll. 859 and 1463). The only specific mention of Statius's *Thebaid*, which is the ultimate source of the entire story, cites the Latin epic, along with "thise bookes olde" (l. 2294), merely as an authority on pagan religious practices.

Allusions in the Miller's Tale are more frequent and employed to very different effect: though less historical, they are more contemporary and literary than those in the first tale. The narrator refers to a saying of Cato (l. 3227) and to a mystery play about Herod (l. 3384). John gives the story of the clerk who fell into a pit (ll. 3457–61)—which betrays no sign of its classical origin in his retelling—and recites a night-spell (ll. 3483–86). Nicholas quotes one of Solomon's proverbs (ll. 3529–30), and the tale as a whole explicitly uses the story of Noah and includes casual citations of several saints. Just as trickery and deceit propel the plot of the Miller's Tale, scholars have discovered its most significant learned references are a series of submerged allusions to popular romances, mystery plays, the *Canticum Canticorum,* and the story of the Annuciation. Because these allusions are parodic as well as hidden, they (unlike the unacknowledged use of Boethius in the Knight's Tale) must be recognized to be effective and then demand interpretation by the reader.

As we have found with other literary contrasts, genre alone cannot account for the different use of allusions in the first two tales. In writing the Knight's Tale, Chaucer eliminated many of the classical references he found in the *Teseida,* but his practice is exactly the reverse in his other ancient romance, *Troilus and Criseyde,* which has many more allusions than its Boccaccian original. Correspondingly, allusions in Chaucer's later fabliaux are very different from those in the Miller's Tale: the Reeve's Tale and the Shipman's have none at all, while those in the Merchant's Tale are much more frequent and more learned, including many that are classical.

Vocabulary is the basic element of any poem, and here also we find a deliberate and sustained contrast between the first two Canterbury tales. Some of the difference is obviously determined by genre, although the purity of each word list can be striking: noble chivalric words like *pitee, honour, adventure, roial, victorie, glorie, chivalrie, conquerour, destynee,* and *pride* occur frequently in the romance, but not once in the fabliau; conversely, words of pleasure and deceit like *joly, gay, derne, solas,* and *sleigh* are relatively common in the fabliau, but are absent from the romance.

Even more revealing, and further proof that Chaucer has given each poem its own special vocabulary, are words that appear in both tales with radically different meanings. *Lord,* for example, is an important term in the Knight's Tale; it occurs twenty-three times, often to describe Theseus and his authority. *Lord* is found three times in the Miller's Tale: once in reference to the Christian God during Nicholas's attempts to convince John of a second flood (l. 3535); once in Absolon's ludicrous description of himself as a "lord at alle degrees" (l. 3724), as he vengefully tries to get Alisoun to offer a second kiss; and once (the only time it approaches its primary meaning in the Knight's Tale) at the end of Alisoun's portrait when we are cynically told she is the right sort to marry a yeoman or "for any lord to leggen in his bedde" (l. 3269). It is easy to imagine that the deceitful, comic, and sexual contexts in which *lord* appears in the Miller's Tale were deliberately chosen because they so accurately define how the second tale differs from the first. Similarly, the word *degree*, which reflects the central concern of the Knight's Tale with order and harmony, appears fifteen times in the romance; its single, comic use in the Miller's Tale is by Absolon when he describes himself as a "lord at alle degrees" (l. 3724). *Mercy* is another key concept in the Knight's Tale; the word occurs twelve times, referring both to the noble virtue (for example, "Fy / Upon a lord that wol have no mercy" [ll. 1773–74]) and, less frequently, to what the courtly lover asks from his lady. Its one appearance in the Miller's Tale, however, is during Nicholas's outrageous parody of courtly speech as he holds Alisoun hard by the haunchbones (l. 3288).

Chaucer's careful use of vocabulary to develop the fundamental literary conflict between the first two tales is shown by two words that have an abstract, idealistic meaning in the romance, but a physical, reductive one in the fabliau. *Olde* appears seventeen times in the Knight's Tale, often to suggest the dignity of the story and its characters by emphasizing their venerable age (for example, ll. 859, 1880, and 2838); the single occurrence of the word in the Miller's Tale, by contrast, stresses the sexual incapacity of old John, which makes Alisoun available and initiates the plot (l. 3225; see the similar use of *elde* at l. 3230). A second such word is *noble,* one of the most important terms in the Knight's Tale, which has itself been described as a pageant of the noble life. *Noble* appears twelve times in the body of the romance, which is then called a "noble storie" in the following link (l. 3111), during which the Miller declares that he, too, will tell a "noble tale" (l. 3126). The single appearance of *noble* in the Miller's Tale, however, perfectly defines its artistic and thematic differences from the romance: in the virtuosic portrait of Alisoun, we are told that her hue was brighter "than in the Tour the noble yforged newe" (l. 3256). A reference to the Tower of London in another context might well suggest chivalry, but here, especially when we remember the use of the word in the first tale, *noble* exposes the contemporary and ruthlessly materialistic world of the fabliau. Although Alisoun's portrait is a comic achievement of great artistic skill, the values it expresses, like the shining appeal of the coin, are directly opposed to the philosophical nobility of the Knight's Tale.

THE THEMATIC DIALECTIC OF THE FIRST TWO TALES

Impressive as both the Knight's Tale and the Miller's Tale are as individual works, they achieve their fullest meaning when read together, as the previous discussion of their contrasting poetics has attempted to show. Chaucer's artistic dialectic makes each of the pair a tool by which to understand better the particular achievements (and limitations) of the other: in Pandarus's terms, each is at once a whetstone and a carving instrument. When the Knight's Tale is read in the light of the very different art of the Miller's Tale, we see more clearly how the idealism of its characterization, the nobility of its imagery and vocabulary, and the philosophical dignity of its speeches all contribute to a straightforward but abstract poetic capable of asking important personal, political, and religious questions. Similarly, the deft comedy and perfection of form that distinguish the Miller's Tale, based on such elements as racy speech, swift transitions, and satiric characterization, stand out all the sharper in contrast to the long and somewhat ponderous Knight's Tale.

The artistic dialectic of the Knight's Tale and the Miller's Tale is more than a literary exercise in stylistic variety, for it leads us to the thematic dialectic between the two tales. Their contrasting, though equally successful, kinds of poetry force the reader to confront two very different visions of the world. The philosophical seriousness of the Knight's Tale is clear enough. Without denying the complexities of this life and despite a few passages that some have taken as comic, the romance is an idealistic epic of ancient heroism that advocates chivalric ideals among men in imitation of a divine Chain of Love. For all its concern with human suffering, the Knight's Tale finds value in the world and order in the universe. The greatest achievement of the Miller's Tale is undoubtedly the delightful perfection of its comedy (whose ability to make readers laugh seems undiminished after nearly six hundred years), yet it, too, offers a vision of the world—and a daring one at that. Modern critics sometimes argue that the Miller's Tale is advocating either rampant sexuality or orthodox Christian doctrine, though it is hard to know which view Chaucer would find more surprising: that he approved of the values of the fabliau or that they are, in fact, essentially religious. Both interpretations minimize the shock of the Miller's Tale by ignoring the questions of morality and taste inevitably raised by juxtaposing such a scurrilous poem to the noble Knight's Tale. That Chaucer himself was aware of the problem is indicated by his two long defenses (ll. 725–46 and 3167–86), which, amidst much characteristic irony, make the serious point that unless he, as poet, includes every word of every kind of story, he must "telle his tale untrewe, / Or feyne thyng" (ll. 735–36) and so "falsen som of my mateere" (l. 3175). Chaucer has slyly turned against itself the standard medieval accusation that poetry is nothing but lies; he insists that truth goes beyond the philosophical idealism of the Knight's Tale and must include even the low doings of the fabliau.

The thematic dialectic of the first two Canterbury tales reveals many things about each that would not be so apparent if the tales were read separately. By placing the Miller's Tale after the Knight's Tale, Chaucer makes us aware of how much has been left out of the romance. The Knight's Tale is a celebration of the possibilities of this life and the achievements of human beings—both appropriate to the pagan setting of the poem. Although he is a mortal man, the admirable Theseus aspires to imitate the divine Chain of Love on earth. The other characters in the poem are similarly shown to be essentially good and capable of moral growth. Hippolyta comes to love and marry her conqueror, while Arcite and Palamon, despite their Theban background, never lose a fundamental chivalric idealism even when their rivalry seems most deadly, and so are capable of final reconciliation.

Attractive as this vision of human nobility is, the Miller's Tale calls it sharply into question. In contrast to the first tale, the second has a shrewd understanding of human appetites and ambition—

from an old man's passion for his young wife to a clerk's itch to fool his *lewed* landlord. Ignoring the urges of the body altogether, the Knight's Tale often sees only the highest potential of men, and so it is left to the Miller's Tale to remind us that, though human beings may aspire to the heavens, they often act basely. By its rustic and animalistic imagery and by speech that is colloquial and deceptive rather than formal and philosophical, the second tale shows us how far from the idealism of romance much of actual life is led. In contrast to the honorable love of Palamon and Arcite, who spend untold years in faithful devotion to the chaste Emelye, the rival truth of the Miller's Tale is perhaps best summed up in a characteristically witty and cruel proverb that explains why Nicholas succeeds with Alisoun while Absolon fails: "Alwey the nye slye / Maketh the ferre leeve to be looth" (ll. 3392–93).

In addition to making us laugh, the fabliau forcefully reminds us how stupid and unfeeling human beings can be and fully illustrates their capacity for self-deception and self-destruction. The Miller's Tale offers a pessimistic view of human rationality in contrast to the Knight's Tale: all of its characters are driven by passion rather than reason, and the only thinking in the tale that is not merely wishful is deceitful. As the special artistry of the Miller's Tale also forces us to recognize, characterization in the Knight's Tale is vague, and its speeches, along with much of the action, abstract. Its noble poet, like Theseus, wants to bring order to the complexities of life, but his solutions, like the symmetrical stadium, are often too neat and simple to be completely satisfying. If the first tale inspires us by expressing the human capacity for heroism and generosity, the second speaks to our fear that men are nothing more than creatures of duplicity and selfish desire, who, for all their cleverness, are incapable of self-control or self-knowledge. After the fabliau, the faith in human achievement and goodness advocated by the romance seems naive indeed.

Of course the dialectic works both ways. If the Miller's Tale exposes limits in the Knight's Tale, the reverse is equally true. The fabliau demonstrates what it would be like if the nobility celebrated by the romance were completely absent—a cruel, harsh world almost totally devoid of kindness or affection, let alone love. For all the brilliance of its narrative surface, its characters reveal the emptiness of a life that is pure appetite. The tale is full of wit and jokes, but its distant narrator, deceitful speech, and mocking laughter, if taken seriously at all, can frighten as well as amuse. As the strict plotting and animalistic imagery make clear, the vision of the Miller's Tale is excessively mechanical and reductive. Attempts to soften its harsh view of life by finding poetic justice in the tale are misleading, for it is the heartlessness of the story, in which a foolish old man is humiliated while his lecherous wife escapes punishment entirely, that makes us laugh. If the Miller's Tale appeared by itself, as is often the case with French fabliaux, the horribleness of its world and people would probably never become a real issue, for the reader would be content to accept the humor for itself. After the idealism of the Knight's Tale, however, it is hard not to ask more serious questions.

In the dialectic between the Knight's Tale and the Miller's Tale, Chaucer trains us to be good readers of poetry. He shows us that we are not to choose between the tales but to learn from both, for each has both moral and aesthetic value. The reader need not try to explain away the immorality of the Miller's Tale or find the stiff idealism of the Knight's Tale more agreeable by detecting an underlying vein of satire; rather, he should explore the achievement and limits of each work as it stands, using the other to help him. Neither of the first two tales is absolutely good or bad in theme or style; each is a provisional work, trying out one approach to art and life, and thus the reader cannot be completely satisfied with either. Because Chaucer is a serious artist as well as a Christian, he avoids pat morals and poems with obvious lessons. Like his contemporaries William Langland and the *Gawain*-poet, Chaucer is more concerned with intelligent moral instruction than indoctrination. Through the variety and contrast of the *Canterbury Tales,* he asks more questions than he provides answers and clearly aims for plenitude and possibility rather than certainty. The method is very exciting, but asks a great deal from us. Chaucer supplies the many different tales, but we must work out their relationships. The first two Canterbury tales announce the impossibility of completely accepting any single tale, any single theme, or any single artist as final. Instead, we are to learn from all the poets of the *Canterbury Tales.*

Chronology

ca.1340–45	Geoffrey Chaucer born, probably in the wine-marketing area of London, Vintry Ward. His parents, Agnes and John Chaucer, are wealthy property owners; John is a prosperous London wine merchant.
1357	Chaucer serves as a page to Elizabeth de Burgh, Countess of Ulster.
1359–60	Chaucer serves in King Edward III's army in France. He is captured, but Edward pays his ransom.
ca.1366	Chaucer marries Philippa Roet. He begins his association with John of Gaunt, probably through his wife, whose sister, Katherine Swynford, is John of Gaunt's mistress. John Chaucer dies.
1367	As a member of King Edward III's household, Chaucer receives a royal annuity.
ca. 1368–71	Writes *The Book of the Duchess*.
ca. 1372–80	Writes *Saint Cecilia*, which later becomes the Second Nun's Tale, and some of the Monk's tragedies.
1372–73	Sent to Genoa and Florence in the service of the king, Chaucer probably becomes acquainted with the writings of Boccaccio, Petrarch, and Dante. He may also have met Petrarch.
1374	Chaucer moves to the house over the gate of Aldgate. Edward III appoints him Controller of the Customs and Subsidies on Wool for the port of London.
1377	Chaucer travels to France on the king's behalf. While he is there, Edward III dies and Richard II becomes king. Richard renews Chaucer's customs appointment and confirms his royal annuity.

1378	Richard II sends Chaucer to Milan, where he renews his acquaintance with Italian literature.
ca.1378–80	Writes *The House of Fame*.
1380	Cecilia Chaumpaigne sues Chaucer for *raptus*. He is cleared of all responsibility.
ca.1380–82	Writes *The Parliament of Fowls*.
1382–85	Chaucer is appointed Controller of the Petty Customs, but then begins to phase himself out of his customs jobs by appointing full-time deputies.
ca.1382–87	Chaucer translates Boethius's *Consolation of Philosophy* and writes *Troilus and Criseyde, Palamoun and Arcite* (the Knight's Tale), *The Legend of Good Women,* and other shorter works.
1385	Appointed Justice of the Peace for Kent.
1386	Chaucer is elected to Parliament as one of the two "Knights of the Shire" to represent Kent. He gives up his house at Aldgate and his controllerships.
1387	Philippa Chaucer dies. Chaucer loses his royal annuity and goes into debt. He travels to Calais.
ca.1387–92	Writes the General Prologue and the earlier of the *Canterbury Tales*.
1389	Richard II appoints Chaucer Clerk of the King's Works.
ca.1390–91	Chaucer oversees construction and repair on several buildings, including the Tower of London, Westminster Palace, and St. George's Chapel at Windsor Castle. Usually carrying substantial amounts of money, he is robbed several times and possibly is injured.
1391	Chaucer relinquishes his clerkship and is appointed deputy forester of the Royal Forest at North Petherton in Somerset.
ca.1391–93	Writes *A Treatise on the Astrolabe*.
ca.1392–95	Writes most of the *Canterbury Tales* during this period.
1394	Richard II grants Chaucer a new royal annuity.
ca.1396–1400	Chaucer writes the latest of the *Tales*, including probably the Nun's Priest's Tale and the Canon's Yeoman's Tale, and several other shorter poems.

1399   John of Gaunt dies. Later in the year, Richard II is deposed and killed; Henry IV becomes king. Henry confirms Chaucer's pension and grants him an additional annuity. Chaucer leases a house in the garden of Westminster Abbey.

1400   Chaucer dies, probably sometime between June and October, and is buried in Westminster Abbey.

Contributors

HAROLD BLOOM, Sterling Professor of the Humanities at Yale University, is the author of *The Anxiety of Influence, Poetry and Repression,* and many other volumes of literary criticism. His forthcoming study, *Freud: Transference and Authority,* attempts a full-scale reading of all of Freud's major writings. A MacArthur Prize Fellow, he is general editor of five series of literary criticism published by Chelsea House. During 1987–88, he served as Charles Eliot Norton Professor of Poetry at Harvard University.

CHARLES MUSCATINE is Professor of English at the University of California at Berkeley. His books on medieval literature include *Chaucer and the French Tradition, Poetry and Crisis in the Age of Chaucer,* and most recently *The Old French Fabliaux.*

E. TALBOT DONALDSON was Professor Emeritus of English at Indiana University at Bloomington. A well-known Chaucerian, he published a major edition of Chaucer's poetry and wrote *Speaking of Chaucer* and *The Swan at the Well: Shakespeare Reading Chaucer.*

DOUGLAS BROOKS is Professor of English at the University of Manchester. He has published articles on various periods of English literature and is the author of *Number and Pattern in the Eighteenth Century.*

ALASTAIR FOWLER is Regius Professor of Rhetoric and English Literature at the University of Edinburgh. His numerous publications include studies of Spenser, an edition of Milton's poetry, and his most recent book, *Kinds of Literature,* a study of genre.

DONALD R. HOWARD was Olive H. Palmer Professor in Humanities at Stanford University and a widely-known medieval scholar.

167

His books include *The Idea of the* Canterbury Tales and *Writers and Pilgrims: Medieval Pilgrimage Narratives and Their Posterity.*

ROBERT W. HANNING is Professor of English at Columbia University. He is the author of *The Vision of History in Early Britain, The Individual in Twelfth Century Romance,* and a translation of the *Lais of Marie de France.*

F. ANNE PAYNE, Professor of English and Medieval Literature at the State University of New York at Buffalo, is the author of *King Alfred and Boethius* and *Chaucer and Menippean Satire.*

HELEN COOPER teaches at Oxford University. Her publications include *Pastoral: Medieval into Renaissance* and *The Structure of the* Canterbury Tales.

C. DAVID BENSON is Professor of English at the University of Connecticut. He is the author of *The History of Troy in Middle English Literature* and *Chaucer's Drama of Style.*

Bibliography

Baldwin, Ralph. *The Unity of the* Canterbury Tales. Copenhagen: Rosenkilde og Bagger, 1955.

Beidler, Peter G. "Chaucer's Knight's Tale and Its Teller." *English Record* 18 (1968): 54–60.

Bishop, Ian. "Chaucer and the Rhetoric of Consolation." *Medium Aevum* 52 (1983): 38–49.

Blake, Kathleen A. "Order and the Noble Life in Chaucer's Knight's Tale?" *Modern Language Quarterly* 34 (1973): 3–19.

Bolton, W. F. "The Topic of the Knight's Tale." *Chaucer Review* 1 (1967): 217–27.

Boitani, Piero. *Chaucer and Boccaccio*. Oxford: Society for the Study of Medieval Language and Literature, 1977.

Brewer, Derek. *Chaucer*. 3d ed. London: Longman Group, 1973.

Burlin, Robert B. *Chaucerian Fiction*. Princeton: Princeton University Press, 1977.

Cameron, Allen B. "The Heroine in the Knight's Tale." *Studies in Short Fiction* 5 (1968): 119–27.

Cooper, Helen. *The Structure of the* Canterbury Tales. London: Gerald Duckworth, 1983.

Cozart, William R. "Chaucer's Knight's Tale: A Philosophical Reappraisal of a Medieval Romance." In *Medieval Epic to the "Epic Theatre" of Brecht*, edited by R. P. Armato and J. M. Spalek. Los Angeles: University of Southern California Press, 1968.

Crampton, Georgia R. *The Condition of Creatures*. New Haven: Yale University Press, 1974.

Curry, Walter Clyde. *Chaucer and the Medieval Sciences*. New York: Barnes & Noble, 1926.

David, Alfred. *The Strumpet Muse*. Bloomington: Indiana University Press, 1976.

Dean, Christopher. "Imagery in the *Knight's Tale* and the *Miller's Tale*." *Medieval Studies* 31 (1969): 149–63.

Donaldson, E. Talbot. *Speaking of Chaucer*. New York: W. W. Norton, 1970.

Elbow, Peter H. "How Chaucer Transcends Oppositions in the Knight's Tale." *Chaucer Review* 7 (1972): 97–112.

Fairchild, H. N. "Active Arcite, Contemplative Palamon." *Journal of English and Germanic Philology* 26 (1927): 285–93.

Foster, Edward. "Humor in the Knight's Tale." *Chaucer Review* 3 (1968): 88–94.

Frost, William. "An Interpretation of Chaucer's Knight's Tale." *Review of English Studies* 25 (1949): 289–304.

Gaylord, Alan T. "The Role of Saturn in the Knight's Tale." *Chaucer Review* 8 (1974): 171–90.

Haller, Robert S. "The Knight's Tale and the Epic Tradition." *Chaucer Review* 1 (1966): 67–84.

Halverson, John. "Aspects of Order in the Knight's Tale." *Studies in Philology* 57 (1960): 606–21.

Harder, Bernhard H. "Fortune's Chain of Love: Chaucer's Irony in Theseus' Marriage Counseling." *University of Windsor Review* 18 (1984): 47–52.

Helterman, Jeffrey. "The Dehumanizing Metamorphoses of the Knight's Tale." *ELH* 38 (1971): 493–51.

Herzman, Ronald B. "The Paradox of Form: *The Knight's Tale* and Chaucerian Aesthetics." *Papers on Language and Literature* 10 (1974): 339–52.

Holtz, Nancy Ann. "The Triumph of Saturn in the Knight's Tale: A Clue to Chaucer's Stance Against the Stars." In *Literature and the Occult,* edited by Luanne Frank. Arlington: University of Texas Press, 1977.

Howard, Donald R. *The Idea of the* Canterbury Tales. Berkeley: University of California Press, 1976.

Hulbert, J. R. "What Was Chaucer's Aim in the *Knight's Tale?*" *Studies in Philology* 26 (1929): 375–85.

Jones, Terry. *Chaucer's Knight.* Baton Rouge: Louisiana State University Press, 1980.

Jordan, Robert M. *Chaucer and the Shape of Creation.* Cambridge: Harvard University Press, 1967.

Justman, Stewart. " 'Auctoritee' and the Knight's Tale." *Modern Language Quarterly* 39 (1978): 3–14.

Kaske, R. E. "The Knight's Interruption of the Monk's Tale." *ELH* 24 (1957): 249–68.

Knight, Stephen. *The Poetry of the* Canterbury Tales. Sydney: Angus & Robertson, 1973.

Kolve, V. A. *Chaucer and the Imagery of Narrative: The First Five Canterbury Tales.* Stanford: Stanford University Press, 1984.

Leach, Eleanor Windsor. "Morwe of May: A Season of Feminine Ambiguity." In *Acts of Interpretation: The Text in Its Contexts, 700–1600: Essays on Medieval and Renaissance Literature in Honor of E. Talbot Donaldson,* edited by Mary J. Carruthers and Elizabeth D. Kirk. Norman, Okla.: Pilgrim, 1982.

Lester, G. A. "Chaucer's Knight and the Medieval Tournament." *Neophilologus* 66 (1982): 460–68.

Loomis, Dorothy Bethurum. "Saturn in Chaucer's Knight's Tale." In *Chaucer und Seine Zeit.* Tubingen: Max Niemeyer Verlag, 1968.

Lumiansky, R. M. "Chaucer's Philosophical Knight." *Tulane Studies in English* 3 (1952): 47–68.

McAlindon, T. "Cosmology, Contrariety and the Knight's Tale." *Medium Aevum* 55 (1986): 41–57.

McCall, John P. *Chaucer Among the Gods.* University Park: Pennsylvania State University Press, 1979.

Mann, Jill. *Chaucer and Medieval Estates Satire*. London: Cambridge University Press, 1973.

Meier, T. K. "Chaucer's Knight as 'Persona': Narration as Control." *English Miscellany* 20 (1969): 11–21.

Muscatine, Charles. "Form, Texture, and Meaning in Chaucer's *Knight's Tale*." *PMLA* 65 (1950): 911–29.

Neuse, Richard. "The Knight: The First Mover in Chaucer's Human Comedy." *University of Toronto Quarterly* 31 (1962): 299–315.

Payne, F. Anne. *Chaucer and Menippean Satire*. Madison: University of Wisconsin Press, 1981.

Payne, Robert O. *The Key of Remembrance*. New Haven: Yale University Press, 1963.

Penninger, F. Elaine. "Chaucer's Knight's Tale and the Theme of Appearance and Reality in the *Canterbury Tales*." *South Atlantic Quarterly* 63 (1964): 398–405.

Root, Robert K. *The Poetry of Chaucer*. Boston: Houghton Mifflin, 1922.

Ruggiers, Paul G. *The Art of the* Canterbury Tales. Madison: University of Wisconsin Press, 1965.

Salter, Elizabeth. *Chaucer: The Knight's Tale* and *the Clerk's Tale*. London: E. Arnold, 1962.

Scheps, Walter. "Chaucer's Theseus and the Knight's Tale." *Leeds Studies in English* 9 (1977): 19–34.

Schmidt, A. V. C. "The Tragedy of Arcite: A Reconsideration of the Knight's Tale." *Essays in Criticism* 19 (April 1969): 107–16.

Schweitzer, Edward C. "Fate and Freedom in the Knight's Tale." *Studies in the Age of Chaucer* 3 (1981): 13–45.

Spearing, A. C., ed. *The Knight's Tale*. Cambridge: Cambridge University Press, 1966.

Stroud, Theodore A. "Chaucer's Structural Balancing of *Troilus* and the Knight's Tale." *Annuale Médiévale* 21 (1981): 31–45.

Tatelbaum, Linda. "Venus' Citole and the Restoration of Harmony in Chaucer's Knight's Tale." *Neuphilologische Mitteilungen* 74 (1973): 649–64.

Thurston, Paul. *Artistic Ambivalence in Chaucer's Knight's Tale*. Gainesville: University of Florida Press, 1968.

Tripp, Raymond. "The Knight's Tale and the Limitations of Language." *Rendezvous* 6, no. 1 (1971): 23–28.

Underwood, Dale. "The First of the *Canterbury Tales*." *ELH* 26 (1959): 455–69.

Van, Thomas A. "Imprisoning and Ensnarement in *Troilus* and the Knight's Tale." *Papers on Language and Literature* 7 (1971): 3–12.

van Boheemen, Christel. "Chaucer's Knight's Tale and the Structure of Myth." *Dutch Quarterly Review of Anglo-American Letters* 9 (1979): 176–90.

Watson, Christopher. "Chaucer's Knight and His Tale." *Critical Review* 22 (1980): 56–64.

Westlund, Joseph. "The *Knight's Tale* as an Impetus for Pilgrimage." *Philological Quarterly* 43 (1964): 526–37.

Williams, George. *A New View of Chaucer*. Durham, N.C.: Duke University Press, 1965.

Acknowledgments

"Order and Disorder" (originally entitled "The Canterbury Tales") by Charles Muscatine from *Chaucer and the French Tradition: A Study in Style and Meaning* by Charles Muscatine, © 1957 by the Regents of the University of California, © 1985 by Charles Muscatine. Reprinted by permission of the University of California Press.

"Keeping Appointments We Never Made" (originally entitled "The Knight's Tale") by E. Talbot Donaldson from *Chaucer's Poetry: An Anthology for the Modern Reader*, edited by E. Talbot Donaldson, © 1958 by the Ronald Press Co. Reprinted by permission.

"The Meaning of Chaucer's Knight's Tale" by Douglas Brooks and Alastair Fowler from *Medium Aevum* 39, no. 2 (1970), © 1970 by the Society for the Study of Mediaeval Languages and Literature. Reprinted by permission.

"Tale of Civil Conduct" (originally entitled "The Tales: A Theory of Their Structure") by Donald R. Howard from *The Idea of the* Canterbury Tales by Donald R. Howard, © 1976 by the Regents of the University of California. Reprinted by permission of the University of California Press.

"The Struggle between Noble Designs and Chaos: The Literary Tradition of Chaucer's Knight's Tale" by Robert W. Hanning from *The Literary Review* 23, no. 4 (Summer 1980), © 1980 by Fairleigh Dickinson University. Reprinted by permission.

"*Sic et Non:* Discarded Worlds in the Knight's Tale" by F. Anne Payne from *Chaucer and Menippean Satire* by F. Anne Payne, © 1981 by the Board of Regents of the University of Wisconsin System. Reprinted by permission of the University of Wisconsin Press.

"An Opening: The Knight's Tale" by Helen Cooper from *The Structure of the* Canterbury Tales by Helen Cooper, © 1983 by Helen Cooper. Reprinted by permission.

"The First Two Poets of the *Canterbury Tales*" by C. David Benson from *Chaucer's Drama of Style: Poetic Variety and Contrast in the* Canterbury Tales" by C. David Benson, © 1986 by the University of North Carolina Press. Reprinted by permission.

Index